YOU HAVE APPROXIMATELY

884 WEEKS FROM

YOUR CHILD'S FIRST

BIRTHDAY UNTIL THE DAY

THEY GRADUATE AND

MOVE OUT.

"TEACH US TO NUMBER OUR DAYS
(OR MAYBE WEEKS)
THAT WE MAY GAIN A HEART OF WISDOM."

PSALM 90:12

ONE AND TWO
PARENTING THROUGH THE "I CAN DO IT" PHASE

www.JustaPhase.com
Published by Orange, a division of The reThink Group, Inc.,
5870 Charlotte Lane, Suite 300,
Cumming, GA 30040 U.S.A.

All Scripture quotations, unless otherwise indicated, are taken from the Holy
Bible, New International Version®, NIV®. Copyright ©1973, 1978, 1984,
2011 by Biblica, Inc.™ Used by permission of Zondervan. All rights reserved
worldwide. www.zondervan.com The "NIV" and "New International Version"
are trademarks registered in the United States Patent and Trademark Office by
Biblica, Inc.™

Other Orange products are available online and direct from the publisher.
Visit our website at www.ThinkOrange.com for more resources like these.
ISBN: 978-1-941259-66-5

©2016 Reggie Joiner and Kristen Ivy
Authors: Reggie Joiner and Kristen Ivy
Contributors: Jon Acuff, Jim Burns, Jean Sumner, Sherry Surratt
Lead Editor: Karen Wilson
Editing Team: Laurin Greco, Elizabeth Hansen

Art Direction: Ryan Boon and Hudson Phillips
Book Design: FiveStone and Sharon van Rossum

Printed in the United States of America
First Edition 2016
1 2 3 4 5 6 7 8 9 10
04/12/16

Copies of this book are available for bulk distribution.
To receive discount pricing go to www.OrangeStore.org.

ONE
— AND —
TWO

PARENTING THROUGH THE
"I CAN DO IT" PHASE

REGGIE JOINER & KRISTEN IVY

FOR SOME

ONE
AND
TWO

THINGS YOU MIGHT SAY . . .

IS THAT RICE OR SNOT?

JUST TRY THIS ONE BITE.

DON'T SIT ON THE CAT.

WHY IS THIS DIAPER UNDER MY PILLOW?

DON'T PUT THAT IN YOUR MOUTH.

THE BATHTUB ISN'T FOR POOPING.

WHY IS MY PHONE CHARGER IN THE BOX OF GOLDFISH CRACKERS?

STOP! WE LEFT THE PACI.

USE YOUR WORDS.

WHY IS IT SO QUIET?

THINGS THEY MIGHT SAY . . .

MY
BULZODER

PLAY
HIGH-PAD

JEDI
LIGHT
SAVER

BUT I

NEED

MY MOMMY
A DONUT
A *REAL* ROCKET SHIP

HOLD
YOU

I LOB YOU

GOOD
PSGETTI!

EAT
MARSHPILLOW

AGAIN!

ENDORSEMENTS

"Not only is the *It's Just a Phase* series of books the most creative and well-thought-out guide to parenting I have ever encountered, these books are ESSENTIAL to my *daily* parenting. With a 13-year-old, 11-year-old, and 9-year-old at home, I am swimming in their wake of daily drama and delicacy. These books are a reminder to enjoy every second. Because it's just a phase."

CARLOS WHITTAKER
AUTHOR, SPEAKER, AND FATHER OF THREE

"As a counselor who works with kids and families, I love the Just a Phase Series. The first three years of a child's life are particularly crucial in terms of cognitive (brain) and social development. This book not only explains what's happening inside the mind of your preschooler, but also how to best respond and meet his needs in a practical way. Every parent should keep this on their shelf as a reminder that this really is a phase, and you don't want to miss it."

HANNAH RINEHART MA, LPC
LICENSED PROFESSIONAL COUNSELOR, FAMILY COUNSELOR, AND SPEAKER

"It doesn't take very long after you have a baby to wonder what in the world you've gotten yourself into. Reggie and Kristen not only show us what to expect after the first year, but they give us some everyday ideas so we don't miss the magic of a single moment. Because nothing is more wonder-full than a one- and two-year-old."

SUE MILLER
EXECUTIVE DIRECTOR OF PRESCHOOL STRATEGY FOR
ORANGE, AUTHOR, SPEAKER, AND VOLUNTEER MOTIVATOR

"We all know where we want to end up in our parenting, but how to get there can seem like an unsolved mystery. Through the *It's Just a Phase* series, Reggie Joiner and Kristen Ivy team up to help us out. The result is a resource that guides us through the different seasons of raising children, and provides a road map to parenting in such a way that we finish up with very few regrets."

SANDRA STANLEY
FOSTER CARE ADVOCATE, BLOGGER, WIFE TO ANDY STANLEY,
AND MOTHER OF THREE

TABLE OF
CONTENTS

PHASE:

A TIMEFRAME IN A KID'S LIFE WHEN YOU CAN LEVERAGE DISTINCTIVE OPPORTUNITIES TO INFLUENCE THEIR FUTURE

ONE
— AND —
TWO

THE PHASE WHEN NOBODY'S ON TIME,
EVERYTHING'S A MESS, AND ONE
EAGER TODDLER WILL INSIST,
"I CAN DO IT."

EXPECT TO BE LATE DURING THIS PHASE.

Maybe you had to wait for your toddler to "do it myself" (just try and stop them). Or maybe they impressively overflowed a clean diaper just as you got into the car. Whatever the reason, this phase will make even the most punctual adult miss the mark occasionally.

YOU CAN ALSO LOOK FORWARD TO A FEW FASHION STATEMENTS.

Expect a few mismatched outfits, magic marker tattoos, sticker collages, and other various states of creative expression. In this phase, you will choose not only your battles, but also which messes will just have to be tolerated.

THE GREATEST TENSION OF THIS PHASE CAN BE SUMMED UP IN THE PHRASE "I CAN DO IT."

Your toddler's struggle for independence has begun. You feel it the first time they try to feed themselves and dump applesauce down the front of their shirt. Just remember, they're not only learning new skills, they're also developing the confidence they need in order to move on to the next phase.

IT'S JUST A PHASE

SO DON'T MISS IT

ONE AND TWO
THE BEST PHASE

BY SHERRY SURRATT

I'm not sure what captivates me more . . . the spontaneous belly laugh or the drooly-mouthed wonder on their angelic face. I can fall in love with a one-year-old faster than they can stink up a room with a saggy diaper. The cherub cheeks and adorably fat thighs draw me in, almost enough to make me overlook their incessantly snotty nose and the permanent marker drawing on the wall. Almost.

It's the mess that gets me. Their little fingers are drawn like magnets to anything they can break or mangle. The moment their fingers become sticky-gooey, an internal signal screams somewhere in their little bodies, *Wipe yourself on something clean and white. Right now!*

Sitting at the dinner table, I see the same look on my granddaughter, Mollie's, face that I saw on her daddy's face so many years ago. It's the look of curiosity that drives a toddler to snatch and smear, squish, then shriek with delight. I glance across to see the look on her mom's face. It reads, *Could I just eat a meal without being completely grossed out, maybe while the food is still reasonably warm?*

It's hard to believe, but yes, that day will come. But not until Mollie has discovered how much pasta her ears will hold or what a bowl of applesauce feels like as it drips down her face, neck, and eventually, to the floor.

Sweet discovery is what this phase is made of. It's what makes patience and endurance such prized commodities for the parent of this age. You are helping your toddler navigate the mess of discovery.

During this phase, your brilliant bundle of exhaustless energy will climb her first stairs, say her first sentence, and begin to test her independence—independence that will be illustrated with piercing shrieks, tantrums, and that foreboding, vehement word: "*No!*"

But within the mess is an indescribable joy. He just toddled his first Frankenstein steps, three in a row, boasting the proud look of an astronaut landing on the moon. She just grabbed a crayon and scribbled her first work of art. Your darling can identify his nose and eyes and ears on command to rousing applause, and you are certain he has the makings of a brain surgeon.

Sweet joy and pride so big it hurts—this is what wells up in the hearts of moms and dads as they watch their one- and two-year-old develop into a little person with opinions and intellect and personality. And as you gaze, you begin to realize what this really means. Not only do you get a ringside seat to watch the beauty of potential form right before your eyes, but you get the joy of helping influence, train, and build who your child will become. Just remember: There will come a day when your once-helpless baby bathes and dresses and feeds himself, but the journey to get there comes with just a little mess along the way.

Sherry Surratt
President and CEO of MOPS International, Speaker,
Author and Grandmother

EVERY TODDLER

1 & 2

SOME USE VERY FEW WORDS.

SOME NEVER. STOP. TALKING.

SOME ALWAYS POOP IN
THE BIG POTTY.

SOME PREFER A
SQUISHY DIAPER.

SOME HAPPILY EAT QUINOA
AND ARTICHOKES.

SOME GO ON A HUNGER STRIKE
IF IT'S NOT A CHICKEN NUGGET.

SOME WEAR ANY OUTFIT
YOU CHOOSE.

SOME WEAR ANY OUTFIT
THEY CHOOSE.

SOME REFUSE TO WEAR
PANTS IN THE HOUSE.

IS UNIQUE

SOME DEMAND TO
BE CARRIED.

SOME RUN SO FAST
YOU CAN'T KEEP UP.

SOME TAKE A TWO-HOUR NAP
EVERY AFTERNOON.

SOME HAVE TO BE BARRICADED IN
THEIR ROOM FOR A TEN-MINUTE
QUIET TIME.

SOME TODDLERS EAT
THEIR PLAY-DOH®
(OKAY, ALL OF THEM DO THAT.)

EVEN WITH UNIQUE TODDLERS—WHICH YOURS MOST CERTAINLY
IS—MOST TODDLERS AT ONE AND TWO HAVE A FEW THINGS IN
COMMON. THIS BOOK WILL SHOW YOU THE CHARACTERISTICS THEY
SHARE SO YOU CAN MAKE THE MOST OF THE "I CAN DO IT" PHASE.

REMEMBER:
WE HAVEN'T MET YOUR TODDLER.

THIS BOOK IS
JUST ABOUT A
LOT OF TODDLERS.

UNDER

PHYSICALLY 1

MENTALLY 2

CULTURALLY 3

STAND

TODDLER **IS** CHANGING

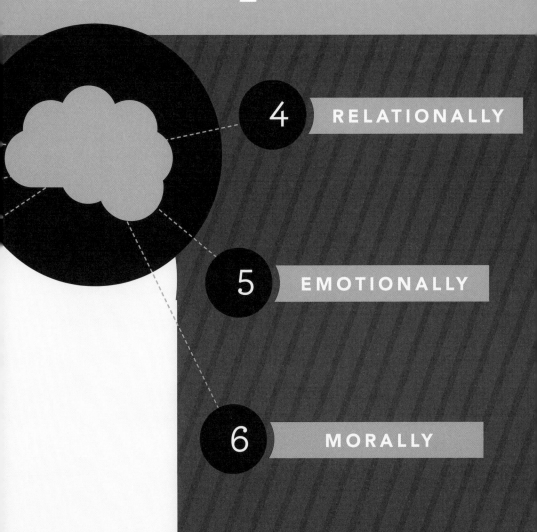

4 RELATIONALLY

5 EMOTIONALLY

6 MORALLY

You have approximately 884 weeks from the time your child turns one

until the day they graduate and move out.

The weeks won't look the same.

Your child is constantly changing.

In the first years of your child's life, it may seem as if they change so

often you will never keep up. Do they require two naps or one? Can you

feed them peanut butter yet? When can they start eating whole grapes?

As a parent, one of your roles is to rediscover your child in each phase—

to pay attention to the changes.

to notice the shifts.

to understand what is new.

WEEKS

Kids in every phase are changing in six ways. By exploring the changes, you might be just a little less shocked, a little less anxious, and even more fascinated by who they are and how they perceive the world.

This section won't solve your most pressing parenting questions— like how to keep your toddler out of the dog's water dish. The next sections will be more practical. First, we want to re-introduce you to the changing human in your home.

SO DON'T MISS
THE PRESENT
REALITIES OF . . .

ONE
— AND —
TWO

one

WHAT'S CHANGING PHYSICALLY

You can't believe it now, but by the end of this phase, you will struggle to remember what your one-year-old looked like on his first birthday. Almost-bald babies grow their first wispy curls of hair. Two-tooth smiles turn into rows of tiny teeth. And pudgy thighs lose their baby rolls as your mostly immobile bundle of joy moves from wobbly toddles to a steady walk and then an all-out run.

While it may seem like these changes happen overnight, they are actually happening week by week, month by month, season by season.

YOUR TODDLER'S SIZE IS CHANGING

Your toddler isn't growing as quickly as she did as a baby. But that doesn't mean she isn't growing. In these two years, your toddler may grow roughly eight inches and gain over ten pounds. That's a 25 percent gain in height and a 50 percent gain in weight!

By two years old, children have achieved about half of their adult height.

TWO-YEAR-OLD HEIGHT

ADULT HEIGHT

If you're curious or anxious about your little one's growth, visit your pediatrician. Well-checks are an important part of monitoring your child's development. Between checkups, you can compare your child's growth to her corresponding growth chart from the World Health Organization.[1]

YOUR TODDLER'S PROPORTIONS ARE CHANGING

Your baby's body, once perfectly suited for crawling, is becoming the body of a delightfully scrappy toddler. His head, which is approximately 80 percent of its adult size, will slow in growth.[2] His body fat, which peaked around his first birthday, is decreasing. His round little belly is disappearing as he develops muscle tone and posture. You might just get a taste of that emerging muscle tone if you try to wrestle a mid-tantrum fifteen-month-old into the car against their will.

Toddlers, pound for pound, are stronger than an ox, particularly in their legs.

YOUR TODDLER'S MOVEMENTS ARE CHANGING

Your toddler may not have the reflexes of a world-class sprinter. She might have slightly less agility and coordination than a member of the national soccer team. But even if she simply watches a ball as it rolls past, don't discount her athletic ability just yet.

The average toddler accomplishes some significant "firsts" in this phase.

»	Walks without assistance	(12-15 months)
»	Walks backwards and sideways	(15-18 months)
»	Scribbles with crayons	(15-18 months)
»	Walks up and down stairs	(18-24 months)
»	Jumps in place	(18-24 months)
»	Throws a ball overhead	(24-36 months)
»	Briefly stands on one foot	(24-36 months)
»	May demonstrate hand preference	(24-36 months)

If you haven't already baby proofed your home, now is a good time to start. You don't have to purchase every gadget on the market, but you should cover the electrical outlets and lock up the cleaning supplies.

two

WHAT'S CHANGING MENTALLY

It doesn't take a Ph.D. in neuroscience to notice that your toddler's brain is growing fast. She is learning a language, discovering how to use new tools (like a spoon), and following simple directions. Your toddler doesn't have a disproportionately large head for nothing.

At birth, the number of synapses (connections between the brain cells) is 2,500 per neuron. But by age two or three it's about 15,000 per neuron. [3]

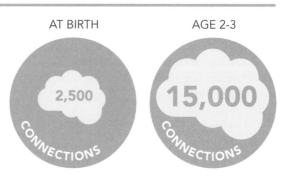

YOUR TODDLER IS SMARTER THAN YOU THINK

You could easily argue that your toddler is the smartest member of your family. Her brain, which was only 25 percent of its adult volume at birth, will grow to 80 percent of its adult volume by her third birthday.[4] And, as if that wasn't enough, brain connections called synapses form faster in this phase than at any other time in life. By age three, your budding genius will have approximately twice as many synapses in her brain as you have in yours—something that allows her to take in information more efficiently than any other non-three-year-old in your family.[5]

In spite of all that growth, you may notice your brainy toddler still struggles to grasp certain concepts.

Generally speaking, toddlers . . .
have difficulty separating fact from fiction.[6]
don't distinguish thoughts from reality.[7]
don't connect the process with the outcome.[8]
(i.e. *It's the same cookie; I just cut it in half.*)

This may make it difficult to reason with your two-year-old. At times she doesn't see things the way you see them because her brain works very differently than yours.

YOUR TODDLER THINKS LIKE AN

ARTIST

Toddlers are not rational, logical thinkers. Instead, these little artists rely on their limited experiences to create general impressions of the world. But even though toddlers make frequent errors in judgment, you can help them learn when you . . .

ENGAGE THEIR SENSES

Below are four ways to engage your toddler's senses and help him learn.

1. TODDLERS LEARN BY DOING
A dancer learns to dance by dancing. A pianist learns by playing. A sculptor learns by sculpting. And toddlers learn just about everything by doing. They learn . . .

noodles drop to the floor ⟶ by dropping them.
fur is attached to the dog ⟶ by pulling it.
metal things taste tangy ⟶ by tasting them.

A toddler's brain grows when they use all five senses.[9] The world is their stage, their instrument, and their canvas. So, they learn best with a little movement, a little music, and a lot of mess.

2. TODDLERS LEARN IN THE PRESENT

As you appeal to your little artist's senses, remember this: What appears to be true right now is the only thing that is true for your toddler. In fact, the only part of his memory that works as efficiently as yours is his "sensory-memory," and that only holds information for a fraction of a second.[10]

3. TODDLERS LEARN IN CATEGORIES

Imagine your artist has a row of buckets he uses to hold his art supplies. In this phase, learning happens when he discovers the characteristics that allow him to sort things. Help your toddler learn by providing opportunities to sort things into categories like . . .
hot / cold
big / little
fast / slow

4. TODDLERS LEARN WITH WORDS

The typical chatty two-year-old adds five new vocabulary words every day.[11]

One of the greatest characteristics of the one- and two-year-old phase is the speed at which they learn words. We will talk more about how to specifically increase your toddler's vocabulary in the next section. But for now remember this: **No matter how chatty or reserved your toddler seems, she can understand a great deal more than she can say, and she's learning fast.**

ONE
AND
TWO

TODDLER TALK

AGE	WHAT THEY SAY

12 MONTHS

"FIRST WORDS"
Pronounces all vowels and about half of the consonant sounds, and says one to four first words—although you may have to translate them

18 MONTHS

NAMING
Points to objects when you name them, often uses body language to communicate, and says 10-50 words—mostly one-syllable nouns that are still more recognizable to parents than strangers

2 YEARS

TWO-WORD SENTENCES
Says 40-200 words including action words such as *go*, pronouns like *me*, and a few words that describe size and location like *little* and *under*

Sometimes says two-word sentences

2 ½ YEARS

THREE-WORD SENTENCES
Says approximately 300 words including a few articles such as *the*, and prepositions like *on*, and beginning to use (sometimes incorrectly) plurals, possessives, and verb tenses

Able to whisper and forms three-part sentences such as: "*Me do it.*"

3 YEARS

GROWING GRAMMAR
Has a word for just about everything and is becoming easier to understand

Answers *What? Where?* and *Why?* questions, and says their name and age when asked

THINGS ABOUT

ONE
— AND —
TWO

A FEW THINGS ABOUT

A FEW THINGS ABOUT ONE *year-olds*

TODDLER HEARING IS BETTER THAN ADULTS'. **THEIR NEW EARS PICK UP ON HIGHER FREQUENCIES AND ARE NOTORIOUSLY MORE SENSITIVE.**

MOST ARE AMBIDEXTROUS. THEY USE BOTH HANDS EQUALLY.

THE FOOT OF A ONE-YEAR-OLD IS ALREADY HALF ITS FUTURE ADULT SIZE.[13]

176

THE AVERAGE ONE-YEAR-OLD TAKES 176 STEPS PER MINUTE. (THAT WILL DROP TO 152 BY THE AGE OF FOUR AND 122 BY THE AGE OF TWELVE.) [12]

33 %

OF KIDS UNDER TWO YEARS OLD CAN ALREADY USE TABLETS.[14]

YOU MIGHT WANT TO KNOW

A FEW THINGS ABOUT TWO
year-olds

EACH YEAR, MORE THAN 500,000 CHILDREN GET EAR TUBES, MAKING THIS THE MOST COMMON CHILDHOOD SURGERY.[15]

YOUR TODDLER WON'T HAVE ANY CLEAR MEMORIES OF THIS PHASE WHEN THEY ARE AN ADULT.[18]

THEY CAN FOLLOW TWO-STEP DIRECTIONS.[17]
(AS LONG AS THE INSTRUCTIONS ARE "GET CANDY FROM THE PANTRY AND EAT IT.")

284.8
A PARENT WILL SPEND APPROXIMATELY 284.8 HOURS PER YEAR SHOPPING AND PREPARING FOOD FOR A TODDLER.
(IT'S A GOOD THING THEY EAT EVERYTHING YOU PREPARE.) [19]

STRANGERS UNDERSTAND 50 PERCENT OF WHAT A TWO-YEAR-OLD SAYS.[16]

three

WHAT'S CHANGING CULTURALLY

In the same way that physical and mental changes happen *to* your child, cultural changes happen *around* your child. At every phase, kids have to adapt to what is changing around them. And sometimes, like in the One and Two Phase, what changes around your child is actually connected to their mental and physical changes.

Consider this. Everything your growing toddler wants to do requires a new skill—from getting dressed to drinking from a cup to using the potty. One moment they can be filled with pride, "I did it!" And the next, they are overcome with frustration.

YOUR TODDLER'S CHANGING ABILITY IS A CRISIS

It isn't a bad crisis. You want your child to discover new abilities. Most parents want their child to eventually . . .
move out of the crib.
drop one of their naps.
ride in a front-facing car seat.
start potty training.

New skills for them mean an increase in freedom for everyone. But it's easy to get preoccupied anticipating the result you want and become impatient with the process. Acquiring new skills takes time. It's a journey riddled with uncertainty, imperfection, and even failure.

Think about the word we use to describe this age: *Toddler*. The very name suggests tension. It's as if someone said, "Sure, they can walk, kind of. But they don't do it well. It's more like a toddle."

For every new skill your toddler learns, you can count on a few unfortunately-timed meltdowns. (You might have a few meltdowns yourself when you walk into a meeting twenty minutes late with yogurt on your shirt.) That's because your culture is changing right along with theirs.

Just remember, on the days that are harder than you anticipated, you love your toddler . . . even if it's deep, deep down. And it's this love that will prove strong enough for both of you.

THE BUFFER IN EVERY CRISIS IS LOVE

Your toddler needs your loving support in order to navigate the crisis of her changing ability. She needs you to stay close and patiently guide her while she works at a new skill. She needs you to clean up the mess when she gets it wrong. She needs you to fill her cup with water when she's thirsty, because no matter how much she wants to, she just can't do that yet. That's why it's important to understand your role as the parent of a toddler.

YOU HAVE ONE ROLE AT THIS PHASE:

EMBRACE

THEIR PHYSICAL NEEDS

Your toddler can't meet all of his needs for himself *just yet*. When you provide an activity, clean up a mess, or offer a snack, you embrace your toddler's physical needs. And as you embrace his needs, you establish that he is safe. Your toddler's feelings of safety now create a foundation for his future relationships, character development, education, and faith.

Your role as a parent will change in the phases to come. But right now, the thing that matters most is how you consistently and lovingly embrace your toddler's physical needs. This role is so significant that we will talk more about how to embrace their needs throughout the rest of this book.

four

WHAT'S CHANGING RELATIONALLY

Have you always wanted a high-maintenance best friend? Do you crave spending time with the emotionally unstable? Are you especially drawn to those who are just a little bit codependent? You've come to the right place. You are parenting in your sweet spot.

You are your toddler's best friend—
his first playmate.
his safe place.

Don't worry: the instability will work itself out. He has you. And quite literally, you are what he needs.

You may have noticed how much he needs you. It's not uncommon for one-year-olds to feel separation anxiety. And toddlers aren't known for their subtlety. If they feel anxiety when you leave, you will know it, probably because they are crying and staring at you wide-eyed as if you abandoned them for life.

Many toddlers struggling with separation anxiety find comfort in a blanket, stuffed animal, or other security object. Having a special blanket won't make your toddler less attached to you or cause future psychological trauma. It will help him feel safe during your absence— just make sure to wash it on occasion and maybe have a spare.[20, 21]

Separation anxiety begins around six months, peaks at fourteen months, and usually resolves by two years.[22]

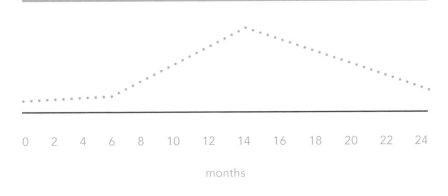

0   2   4   6   8   10   12   14   16   18   20   22   24

months

Mastering separation is just one more of your toddler's changing abilities. Some days will be easier than others. The best way to help your toddler is to embrace her physical needs when she is with you, and to allow her to experience your consistent return after periods of absence.

Your toddler doesn't just crave your physical presence. She also craves your approval. When she puts her shoes on the wrong feet. When she tries to shampoo her own hair—using the entire bottle of shampoo—she will look to you. She will have one primary question in this phase.

YOUR TODDLER WANTS TO KNOW,

"AM I ABLE?"

That's why she climbs the stairs and looks back to see if you are watching. That's why she picks up a crayon and looks to see whether you are smiling or scowling. Your toddler wants your approval.

That may sound like a ridiculous statement. Sure, some toddlers will see your scowling face and turn right back around to color on the wall anyway. Sometimes toddlers want to know they are able—in spite of you. But just before age two, children begin to understand that their behavior influences the adults around them. When that happens, they begin to actively seek adult approval while avoiding adult disapproval.[23]

Toddlers—even the most stubborn and seemingly self-governed ones— want adult approval. They want you to believe in them so they can believe in themselves. They want you to show them they are able.

This innate desire for adult approval is what makes toddlers especially sensitive to shame in this phase. Rather than motivating your toddler to try again, shame causes your toddler to feel alone and incapable. Shame is an intensely painful emotion. Toddlers who feel excessive shame are less able to gain new skills because they are less willing to risk the failure that is a necessary part of any learning process.

"The antidote to shame is empathy."

BRENE BROWN

It's interesting that in the phase when a child is most sensitive to shame, they are also developing an awareness that other people are "like me."[24] They are watching you to see what it means to be human. One of the simplest ways to combat feelings of shame for your toddler is to empathize with him.

When he spills, let him know you sometimes spill, too.
When he feels frustrated, let him know you sometimes feel frustrated, too.
When he isn't sure he can make it to the bathroom on time . . . well.

You increase a toddler's ability to handle challenges when you let them know they aren't alone. Stated another way, you capture their heart when you . . .

DEVELOP THEIR CONFIDENCE

There are many ways you can bolster your toddler's confidence. You are probably already doing most of them—at least some of the time. Developing a toddler's confidence simply means responding to their changing needs and abilities.

That happens every time you . . .
choose tasks based on their ability.
talk to them about what you see them doing.
respond to their emotional cues.
take their perspective.
affirm, praise, and show affection.
avoid harsh words and rejection.[25]

That may seem like an obvious list. What parent would intentionally give their toddler a task they know is far too difficult? But in a phase where your growing toddler tests your patience and your will, it's easy to forget that simple things matter more than you realize. Research has actually linked the strategies above to:

» Improved brain development
» Improved language development
» Improved behavior
» Increased IQ
» Increased early reading [26]

Just remember, toddlers are in process. Don't worry. This isn't the end of the road. There will come a day when your relationship involves more intelligible conversations and a wider variety of music. But for now, just remember you are developing the confidence they need for the phases to come.

POTTY TRAINING

ONE
AND
TWO

RESEARCH HAS FOUND NO DIFFERENCE IN THE METHOD OF POTTY TRAINING USED AND THE LIKELIHOOD OF LATER CHILDHOOD WETTING PROBLEMS.[27]

START WHEN THEY ARE READY

Most toddlers are ready to potty train between 27 and 32 months.
Your toddler may be ready to begin when . . .

» their diaper stays dry for two hours+.
» they tell (or show) you when they need to go.
» they are bothered when their diaper is dirty.
» they can pull their pants off and back on.
» they can understand and follow directions.

PLAN AHEAD

Before you get started, you may want to . . .

» purchase a toddler potty or potty seat.
» check out a potty training book to read together.
» clean the bathroom.
(You will spend a lot of time in there.)

IN CASE YOU HAVEN'T RECEIVED ENOUGH ADVICE, HERE ARE FIVE PRACTICAL SUGGESTIONS TO HELP GUIDE YOU THROUGH THIS PARENTING RITE OF PASSAGE WITH AS FEW CARPET STAINS AS POSSIBLE.

CELEBRATE

Whether you make a chart for stickers or do a potty dance or call all the relatives so they can say, "Good job," make sure to celebrate the successes—no matter how small.

WHILE TRAINING DON'T ASK, **"DO YOU NEED TO POTTY?"** IN THIS PHASE, THE ANSWER WILL ALMOST ALWAYS BE **"NO."**

PREPARE FOR ACCIDENTS

Accidents will happen. Help your toddler not to feel ashamed by letting him know, "Accidents happen, and that's okay." You might even share a personal story of when you accidentally spilled a drink or made a mess.

KEEP THE NIGHTTIME DIAPER

Let your toddler experience daytime success before you tackle the nighttime. Trying to take on too much too fast will only discourage you and your child. Even if you know someone whose fifteen-month-old stays dry all night—it's okay if you move at a different pace.

* THERE'S MORE. WE'VE LISTED A FEW OF OUR FAVORITE RESOURCES ON POTTY TRAINING ON PAGE 127.

five

WHAT'S CHANGING EMOTIONALLY

Somewhere around fifteen months, you become aware that things are changing for your toddler emotionally—about every three minutes. There are moments of thrilling wonder. And there are moments when you may gape open-mouthed at the display of rage that has taken hold of your child. You may find yourself asking, "Is that a happy scream, or are they angry?"

Toddlers feel emotions to an extreme. They aren't just happy, they are *ecstatic*. They aren't just sad, they are *distraught*. They aren't just angry, they are . . . well, get out of the way if you don't want to get bitten.

Toddlers are also beginning to feel new emotions. Around the age of two, when toddlers discover the connection between their actions and the emotions of others, they begin to develop complex emotions like pride, embarrassment, guilt, and shame.[28] But in spite of all the new and intense emotions toddlers feel, they have one significant challenge.

YOUR TODDLER FEELS MORE THAN HE SAYS

Toddlers experience strong feelings before they develop the ability to name them. Even though your toddler will have an explosion of new vocabulary in this phase, don't be surprised if he has very few words for emotions.

Your toddler will continually get better at naming and controlling his emotions. But he needs you to guide him. Embracing your toddler's physical needs in this phase will often mean guiding his emotional needs as well. You are a translator to bridge the gap between his emotions and his vocabulary.

18 Months	May say their first emotion words, like *"happy."* You can help them practice these words by mirroring facial expressions to help them understand.[29]
2 Years	May begin referring to their own emotions by saying things like, *"I'm happy."*[30] You can foster their growing awareness by asking questions like, "Are you happy?"
2 ½ Years	Uses more words for their everyday emotions.[31] Toddlers recognize and name happiness first and most accurately.[32] Next, they name sadness, then hurt, sleepiness, or disgust.[33] Toddlers name anger and fear last.[34]
3 Years	May begin to name not only their own emotions, but also the feelings they see in others.[35] They also recognize what causes their feelings. They know they're happy when they get what they want and sad when they don't.[36, 37] They often fail to see how their emotions affect others.[38]

YOUR TODDLER EXPERIENCES YOUR EMOTIONS

Your toddler watches you. In fact, you've never had anyone watch you so closely. You may lock yourself in the bathroom occasionally just to escape all the watching—and even then, they sit outside and bang on the door.

Your toddler also watches you for social cues. Toddlers are most fascinated by people's feelings, thoughts, and motives.[39] They are in the process of discovering they are a person. And who is better able to teach them what that means than you—a grown-up person?

Studies show, for example, that toddlers are more likely to play with a new toy if their parent smiles when the toy is introduced. They are learning how to respond to other people, objects, and situations by observing how you respond.[40]

The idea of a little person watching your every emotion is stressful. But toddlers are particularly sensitive to stress[41]—so relax. If you want to embrace your toddler's needs, you need to take care of your own needs first. If you want to help him develop emotionally, look for ways to keep your own sanity intact.

six

WHAT'S CHANGING MORALLY

Your toddler is selfish. Sure, that's obvious. He probably doesn't always share without being asked. But you might actually be surprised by all the ways his moral abilities are developing.

YOUR TODDLER IS MORALLY AWARE

Studies of toddlers actually show some fascinating things about the phenomenon of toddler morality.

In one study, eighteen-month-olds watched a researcher eat snacks. The researcher ate goldfish crackers and responded with disgust. Then she ate broccoli and responded with delight. When the toddler was then asked to give the adult some more, toddlers overwhelmingly responded by giving the researcher the food she preferred—*even though the toddlers disliked the broccoli themselves.*[42]

Research like this shows that even at eighteen months old, toddlers are socially smart and capable of compassion.

YOUR TODDLER'S MORAL REASONING IS LIMITED

There's a reason you feel like your toddler still has a little more growing to do in this area. A toddler can't reason morally beyond their ability to reason intellectually. Their moral abilities have some limits.

They can't name the cause for other people's emotions . . .
so they can't fully empathize.
They are inaccurate at connecting motives to actions . . .
so they are overly critical of themselves and others when mistakes happen.
They value action more than words . . .
so they don't always comprehend "lying."[43, 44]
They don't comprehend time . . .
so it's hard for them to wait.

Even with these limits, your toddler's morality isn't static. She is developing, and you can help.[45] The way you embrace your toddler's needs will coach her moral abilities. But first you need to understand this:

YOUR TODDLER IS MOTIVATED BY

SAFETY

If you want to coach your toddler's moral abilities, she needs you to embrace her needs to help her feel safe. You do this when you . . .

RESPOND CONSISTENTLY

Toddlers who feel safe and confident with their caregiver are more advanced in their conscience development.[46] In fact, caregiver support in this phase increases the part of the brain responsible for memory, emotional processing, and stress regulation.[47]

So take each day as it comes. You are training a little human. And the best thing you can do for them is to show up to give them a safe place and a loving context. The next section of this book will get a little more practical about what that means.

ONE AND TWO

May walk without assistance

Says one to four "first words"

Separation anxiety peaks

Walks backwards and sideways

Scribbles with crayons

Jumps in place

Says around 10-50 words, including words for emotions, like *happy*

May drop morning nap

15 MONTHS

18 MONTHS

ONE
TO ...

EMBRACE

AT A GLANCE

DEVELOP THEIR CONFIDENCE	IS MOTIVATED BY SAFETY	RESPOND CONSISTENTLY

Grows to approximately ½ their adult height

Throws a ball overhead

Makes two-word sentences

Can follow two-part instructions

Resolves separation anxiety (for the most part)

May be ready to begin potty-training (look for signs of readiness)

Strangers understand about 50% of what they say

May demonstrate hand preference

2 YEARS

2 ½ YEARS

THREE

THEIR PHYSICAL NEEDS

LEVE

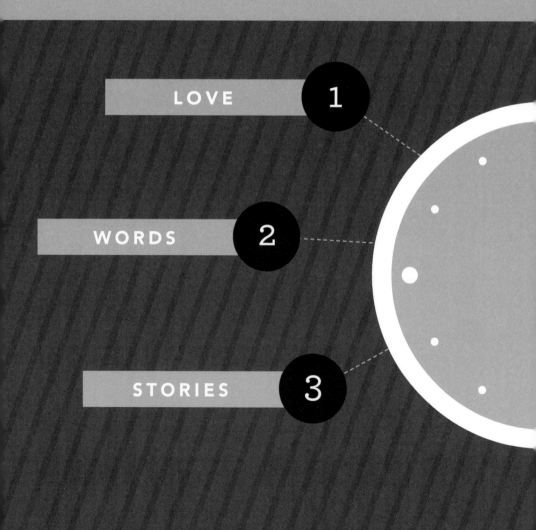

THE SIX THINGS YOUR

1 **LOVE**

2 **WORDS**

3 **STORIES**

RAGE

TODDLER NEEDS

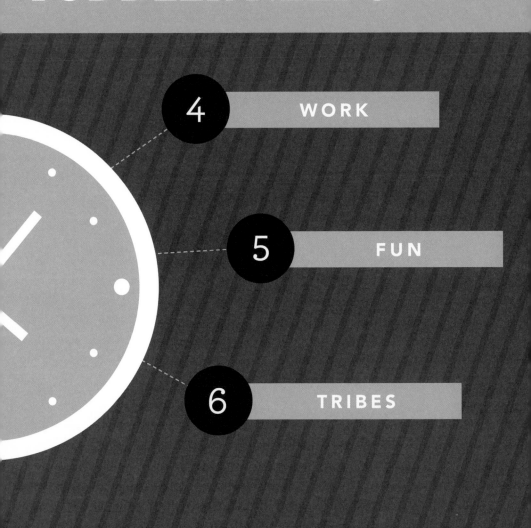

4   WORK

5   FUN

6   TRIBES

Over the next 884 weeks your child will change, but some of their needs will stay the same.

Let's simplify it.

Every child at every phase needs six things.

Before you hit the panic button, these six things are actually pretty simple (a lot simpler than trying to keep the car seat clean and crumb free). And when you give your child these six things through every phase, you will do something meaningful. You will build history together. You will pass on an everyday faith. You will give them a sense of WORTH, DIRECTION, PERSPECTIVE, PURPOSE, CONNECTION, and BELONGING.

WEEKS

But just because every kid at every phase needs the same six things doesn't mean the way you give your child those things stays the same at every phase.

You will constantly redefine how you give your child LOVE, WORDS, STORIES, WORK, FUN, and TRIBES.

This section contains practical suggestions for giving your toddler these six things right now, while they are one and two years old.

SO DON'T MISS
THE DISTINCTIVE
OPPORTUNITIES OF . . .

ONE
— AND —
TWO

TIME

MATTERS

When we wrote the book *Playing for Keeps*, we challenged parents with a meaningful task. We gave them a jar filled with 936 marbles and asked them to reduce the number of marbles in the jar to the actual number of weeks their child had left at home before graduation. (For a one-year-old, that's about 884 marbles.) Their next long-term assignment was to remove one marble each week.

For those parents, the jar became a constant visual reminder of something that's absolutely essential if you want to influence a kid or teenager: TIME.

There's nothing special about a jar of marbles. But something happens when you put a number to the time you have left with your kid.

When you see how much time you have left, you tend to do more with the time you have now.

884 marbles may seem like a lot. Right now, it may seem like your child will never poop in the potty. Mealtimes, where you actually eat instead of

keeping your toddler from feeding the dog, feel like light years away. And the idea of high school graduation simply hadn't crossed your mind—yet.

But 884 weeks will go by fast.

We're not trying to depress you, or tell you to love every single precious moment—including the temper tantrums. But here's the truth:

You will only know your toddler once as a curious, on-the-go one-year-old. Then she will turn two. And before you know it, she will be riding a tricycle and asking you to listen while she counts to one hundred.

Putting a visual number to the time you have left isn't a new idea. One wise leader said it this way:

"Teach us to number our days, that we may gain a heart of wisdom."

PSALM 90:12

So how does counting your days give you a heart of wisdom?
We're not sure.
But we can guess.

Think about what happens with the countdown clock in a basketball game. As the clock gets closer to zero, the intensity increases. The players become more focused.

In the same way, visualizing the time you have with your kid may help you . . .
pace yourself,
narrow your focus,
guard your margin,
value quality interaction,
and become more intentional about what you do.

When you see how much time you have left,
you tend to value what happens over time.

The jar of marbles is also a reminder of the potential you have when you invest in your child over multiple weeks.

What you do this week matters, but you can't get it all done this week. That's why it takes a collection of weeks to parent a child.

This year you will invest a lot of hours into simply keeping your toddler fed, clean, rested, and out of the street in their birthday suit. But if you begin now giving them **love, words, stories, work, fun, and tribes,** over time, these six things will . . .
gain collective momentum.
make history.
build a legacy.

So count down the number of weeks you have with your toddler before their graduation day.

Hint: If you want to cheat, download the free "Legacy Countdown" app and enter your child's birthday. The app will show you an accurate number of weeks specifically calculated for your toddler.

Once you know the number, select a container and fill it with the appropriate number of marbles, coins, paper clips, M&Ms®, jelly beans, gum balls, etc. (Warning: Edible items may disappear faster than one a week.)

Then create a family ritual of removing one item from the container each week as a simple reminder that . . .
time is moving,
every week counts,
and the collection of weeks will influence your child more than you can understand right now in the One and Two Phase.

6 THINGS KIDS NEED OVER TIME

1   LOVE/TIME =
WORTH

2   STORIES/TIME =
PERSPECTIVE

3   FUN/TIME =
CONNECTION

4   WORDS/TIME =
DIRECTION

5   WORK/TIME =
SIGNIFICANCE

6   TRIBES/TIME =
BELONGING

one

LOVE/TIME = WORTH

BE PHYSICALLY AND CONSISTENTLY PRESENT

"A toddler believes that if you love a person, you stay with that person 100 percent of the time."

LAWRENCE BALTER

Of course you love your toddler. That sticky grin. Those chunky thighs. With every passing year, you are discovering new things to love about her. But if you want your child to grow up knowing you love them, you have to prove it—over time. Every kid needs adults who love them in a way that convinces them they are worth something. And the way you consistently prove your love over time will give your child a healthy sense of worth. Below are three practical ways to show love to your toddler.

SHOW UP

It's impossible not to show up—especially when they are clinging to your leg crying for you to, "Hold you." Remember, separation anxiety peaks during this phase. Toddlers need a familiar face in order to feel safe.

There really is no substitute for your presence. Studies show that loving support from caregivers during this phase affects the structure of a child's brain in the years to come. Kids who have consistent care as one- and two-year-olds grow up to have better memory and stress regulation.[48]

That's not to say that you can never leave. You will inevitably have some time away from your toddler during these 104 weeks. When you do leave, whether for work or just your own sanity, here are a few suggestions to help ease the time apart:

» Keep your goodbye short and sweet.
» When you return, spend the first fifteen minutes together.
» When your child isn't with you, let them stay with someone familiar.

In the space below, make a short list of adults who will care for your child when you are away. Take the time to get to know these adults. If possible spend time with them while your child is present.

....

....

....

KNOW THEM

Your toddler isn't like every toddler. **So the way you show up and love your toddler won't be exactly like anyone else.**

Some toddlers like to cuddle.
Some toddlers tell you to "sit over there."

Some toddlers squish their fingers into everything.
Some toddlers throw a fit if their hands get dirty.

Some toddlers take two naps until their third birthday.
Some toddlers insist they "aren't tired" and won't nap.

When it comes to loving your toddler, it's more about knowing what works for the two of you than it is about following any prescribed formula.

Write down a few things about your one-of-a-kind toddler.
YOU MAKE US LAUGH WHEN YOU . . .

....

....

....

YOU GET MOST FRUSTRATED WHEN . . .

....

....

....

SOMETHING THAT MAKES YOU UNIQUE IS . . . :

....

....

....

SET BOUNDARIES

Sometime around fifteen months your precious angel will do something that shocks you. Up until that moment, you may have been under the impression your child was obedient by nature. Wrong. They were a baby. Now they are a toddler. Toddlers test the limits. And parents of toddlers scramble to figure out discipline—fast.

No one plans ahead for that first discipline moment. It sneaks up on you as silently as that little person sitting in your pantry tasting the dog food.

This page won't solve all your discipline problems. For more discipline resources, check out our list of recommendations on page 128. But since you will need a discipline plan before you pick up another book, **here are ten ideas to help you get started:**

1 **Know their limits.** You can often prevent misbehavior. Don't expect your toddler not to grab the shiny, penny within their reach. Toddlers are also better behaved when they have a routine to their day, have had adequate rest, and aren't hungry . . . but you already knew that.

2 **Have a few clear rules.** Your toddler can't remember 182 guidelines for behavior. Instead, have two or three rules like, "Obey right away" and, "Always be kind." Talk about the rules when your child isn't misbehaving.

3 **Give a warning.** Warnings cue your toddler to recognize her own behavior, set expectations, self-correct, and make a better choice.

4 **Be consistent.** If you threaten a consequence, follow through. (Don't threaten what you aren't willing to do—never let a toddler call your bluff.)

5 **Be specific.** When correcting a behavior, use simple, clear, and specific words. Say things like, "You can't bite another person. Biting is not kind."

6 **Reinforce positive behavior.** Catch your child doing something good. When he obeys, say, "Thank you for obeying right away!"

7 **Don't discipline mid-tantrum.** Toddlers in the throes of an emotional outburst are not teachable. Help them gain control before disciplining.

8 **Consider the motive.** Toddlers often cannot express their desires in words. Try to read the situation. Every behavior has a reason behind it.

9 **Correct the behavior without shaming the child.** Be firm and calm. Get on your child's level, look her in the eye and restate the rule. Focus on the unacceptable behavior, not on an unacceptable child. Say things like, "I love you. I don't like what you just did." Use your tone and body language to communicate love and care.

10 **Practice self-discipline.** Your ability to discipline well is dependent on your own emotional health. Get rest. Eat well. Take time for yourself. [49]

two

WORDS/TIME
= DIRECTION

SPEAK THE WORDS THEY NEED TO HEAR

"Anyone who thinks the art of conversation is dead ought to tell a child to go to bed."

ROBERT GALLAGHER

As a parent, you use words to encourage, discipline, and comfort. You use words to describe your child's abilities, character, and personality. Over time, the words you say *to* your child and *about* your child will shape how he sees himself. Maybe that's why James, the brother of Jesus, said that words are like a bridle on a horse or a rudder on a ship. Words over time impact a person's direction. In this section are three practical ways to improve your vocabulary now so you can begin speaking the words your toddler needs to hear.

IMPROVE YOUR PRACTICAL VOCABULARY
In the phases to come, your child will use words to think. That means that the more words they know, the more they can understand and imagine. Perhaps the most practical gift you will give your child in this phase is words.

Talk to your toddler. The greatest way to boost a toddler's vocabulary, communication skills, and confidence is to talk to them. Talk about what you see. Talk about what you do. Talk about what you feel. Name family members and common objects. Experts say that children from "talkative homes" are exposed to as many as 30 million more words when they enter kindergarten than toddlers from non-talkative homes.[50]

When talking to your toddler, keep your words simple, your phrases short, and use repetition. If you want even more ideas on how to accelerate your toddler's practical vocabulary, consider the following:

12 - 18 Months
» Play non-verbal copying games (You pick up a block, they pick up a block.)
» Play cooperative games (Roll a ball back and forth.)
» Give your toddler options ("Do you want an apple or banana?")
» Play identification games ("Where's your . . .? ")

18 - 24 Months
» Repeat what they say and add words
» (When they say "grape," you say, "you want some grapes?")
» Read "first words" books together
(Point to the pictures and let your toddler name what they see.)
» Repeat short phrases throughout the day ("snack time")
» Use facial expressions and body language to act out action words or emotion words when you say them
» Say nursery rhymes or make up rhymes for fun

24 - 36 Months
» Talk about opposites (big / little, more / less, up / down)
» Read *Go. Dog. Go!* Point to the dogs as you describe them
Ask, "Which dog is under the house?" etc.
» Model bigger and better sentences
» Sing songs and play games
("Ring Around the Rosie," "Hokey Pokey," or "London Bridge")
» Tell familiar stories and skip a part or say the wrong thing
» Pause to see if your child fills in the right information

Like everything else, toddlers learn language at different paces. If you are concerned about your toddler's progress, talk with your pediatrician.

As your toddler's vocabulary improves, they will say some sweet, funny, and memorable things. Write some of the fun things your toddler says as a one- and two-year-old below.

....

....

....

....

....

IMPROVE YOUR RELATIONAL VOCABULARY

Toddlers value actions over words. Even with an exploding vocabulary, your toddler doesn't always accurately interpret your words. They also say words before they even know their meaning. This means the best relational vocabulary you have may be your body language, facial expressions, tone, and touch.

Toddlers need to talk about their feelings. Talking with your toddler about their feelings will help them feel understood and secure.[51] Not only can you interpret what they are feeling now, but you can also shape how they think about those emotions in the future. Maybe that's why studies have shown that when mothers talk to children about their feelings during conflict at age two-and-a-half, these children have a stronger conscience at age three.[52] As your toddler learns hundreds of new words, make sure some of them are words that name emotions.

You also strengthen your toddler's relational vocabulary when you . . .
play face to face.
look when they point.
respond when they call.
work together on a cooperative task.
talk about emotions—after they happen.

With older toddlers, you may also offer them strategies to help them manage their extreme emotions. For example, when they are feeling angry or sad, stay calm and say, "Let's take five deep breaths." When they are frustrated that they didn't get their way, give two alternative options they can choose from—so they have a say in what happens next.

IMPROVE YOUR SPIRITUAL VOCABULARY

In the same way your child will use words to think, your child will use words to think about God and about faith. So use some basic faith vocabulary in your home.

Talk about God. Say things like, "Look at the tree that God made" or, "Who made your belly button? God made your belly button."

Talk about church. Say things like, "That is a church" and, "Did you go to church?" Using words like *God, church, Jesus, pray,* and *Bible* with your toddler will give them the foundation for spiritual conversations in the phases to come.

Sing songs. Another way to begin your toddler's spiritual vocabulary is through song. Simple melodies can put spiritual vocabulary in a calm and loving context.

You don't have to be a good singer. You don't even have to be able to hold a tune for your toddler to enjoy the sound of your singing voice. (That might not be true by the end of this phase.)

Singing can be fun when you greet your toddler in the morning, during bath time, or as a lullaby just before bed. So sing!

" Sing songs you remember from your childhood.
" Buy an album or look up songs online.
" Make up a song as you go.

Or simply use one of these: "Jesus Loves Me," "Taps (Day is Done)," "Jesus Loves the Little Children," or "Amazing Grace."

three

STORIES/TIME
= PERSPECTIVE

SELECT STORIES TO INSPIRE THEM

"If you want your children to be intelligent, read them fairy tales. If you want them to be more intelligent, read them more fairy tales."

ALBERT EINSTEIN

If words influence a kid's direction, stories over time shape a kid's perspective. Think about your own life. You grew up listening to stories—stories your parents or mentors told, stories you heard on TV, in books, movies, or video games, and maybe even a few Bible stories. In every phase of your kid's life, stories shape how they think about the world and their place in it.

HIGHLIGHT CULTURAL STORIES

Your toddler is still a little young for the latest blockbuster movie or video game, so the best cultural stories at this phase are books. Some days it may feel like one more round of "mooing" and "quacking" will make you swear off books forever. But research shows that reading to toddlers strengthens their growing brain and increases their vocabulary.[53]

YOUR READING LIST →

BOOKS

Look for books with **rhymes, repetition, and only a few words** on each page. Stories that involve animals, transportation and silliness are favorites in this phase. Below are some suggestions to get your started:

MR. BROWN CAN MOO, CAN YOU? *Dr. Seuss*	DUCK ON A BIKE *David Shannon*	ARE YOU MY MOTHER? *P.D. Eastman*
LLAMA LLAMA RED PAJAMA *Anna Dewdney*	GO, DOG. GO! *P.D. Eastman*	BLUEBERRIES FOR SAL *Robert McCloske*
IF YOU GIVE A MOUSE A COOKIE *Laura Joffe Numeroff*	GREEN EGGS AND HAM *Dr. Seuss*	CLICK, CLACK, MOO: COWS THAT TYPE *Doreen Cronin*
MADELINE *Ludwig Bemelmans*	FEELINGS *Aliki*	CAPS FOR SALE *Esphyr Slobodkina*
GOODNIGHT, GOODNIGHT, CONSTRUCTION SITE *Sheri Duskey Rinker*	PETE THE CAT: I LOVE MY WHITE SHOES *Eric Litwin*	DON'T LET THE PIGEON DRIVE THE BUS *Mo Willems*

When selecting books to read together, choose books with pictures and only a few words per page. As you read, pause and have a conversation. With younger toddlers, ask simple questions like, "Where are Pete's shoes?" As your toddler gets older, make your questions more open ended. Ask things like, "Why is Llama crying?"

What are some of your toddler's favorite books to read together?

....

....

....

CAPTURE FAMILY STORIES

Toddlers love to hear stories about themselves. Actually, there's a purpose for retelling stories about your toddler. Developmental scientists have shown that when parents tell stories about their toddler's recent experiences, toddlers remember the experience longer and gain insight into people's feelings and motives.[54] So tell stories about your day while you're doing other activities—like bath time, morning time, or cuddle time. You can also inspire your toddler to tell family stories by creating a small photo album with pictures that prompt them to talk about family members and events.

Create a family archive. It's hard to believe it, but you won't remember this phase in a year or two. Even if you aren't a scrapbooking, journaling type, you can record something about this phase. You don't have to do it all. But choose one or two things that you can do this year.

» Make handprints or footprints.
» Start a journal written to your child.
» Record things your toddler says in a smart phone app.
» Fill a shoebox with keepsakes.
» Take pictures—even if you don't have the time or money to print or frame them now.

There's no shortage of ways to document the first years of a baby's life. If you want a little assistance, here are a few tools to help you:

Go online and check out websites like: *Momentific*, *Shutterfly*, or *Peekaboo*. Download apps like: *1 Second Everyday*, *ShutterCal*, *Moment Garden*, *Tiny Beans*, *Bambio*, or *My iStory*.

How have you recorded other memorable events in your past? What are some things you want to remember about your toddler in this phase, and how can you do that?

....

....

....

SHARE FAITH STORIES

Your eighteen-month-old isn't going to recite the twenty-third Psalm. But that doesn't mean he's not ready to interact with the Bible stories you know and love. Don't worry about reading word-for-word from Scripture right now. Instead look for individual Bible stories retold for toddlers and preschoolers. As you select Bible stories, choose stories that will capture his imagination about a really big God. You might start with these:

» The Creation Story
» The Christmas Story
» The Easter Story[55]

Look for the same qualities your toddler enjoys in other stories: **rhyming, repetition, pictures, and only a few words per page.**

Keep in mind toddlers tend to focus on one thing at a time. They may be overly interested in "that silly snake in a tree" and miss the point of the story entirely. Don't get discouraged. Your child's understanding of Bible stories will grow as he does.

four

WORK/TIME
= PURPOSE

GIVE THEM PRACTICAL RESPONSIBILITIES

"The fundamental job of a toddler is to rule the universe."

LAWRENCE KUTNER

It probably seems too early to talk about work. Your toddler certainly isn't getting a paycheck—although that would be helpful. And there's a good chance you aren't creating a chore chart for your one-year-old. But your toddler is developing confidence. Work creates opportunities for refining skills, discovering abilities, and cultivating resilience. The work your child does over time will give him a sense of purpose. Below are three ways to think about work in the One and Two Phase.

GIVE THEM SOMETHING TO DO
You will want to do everything for your toddler for two reasons.

1.   It will be five times faster.
2.   It will be approximately 99.7 percent less messy.

Your toddler needs to do some things for herself. There may be times when you should let her . . .
feed herself tomato soup with a spoon,
dress herself in rainboots when it's sunny,
or brush her hair even if it ends up with more tangles.

Watch for signs of readiness. If your toddler wants to try something within reason, let her. If the task proves to be too challenging, step in and help. Offer a simpler task to bolster her confidence to try again.

Add to this list. What can your one- or two-year-old do? When did you discover they could do it?

....

....

....

....

....

....

GIVE THEM SOMETHING TO OWN

If your toddler knows numbers at all, there's a good chance he still counts, "One, two, seven, five!" That would make him a pretty unreliable banker.

While toddlers can't count consistently or understand money (just ask how much they think something costs), they can learn a few basic concepts that will prepare the way for future financial responsibility. For example, it's not too soon to let your toddler know . . .
you need money to buy things.
you get money by working.
sometimes you have to wait to buy something you want.

Delayed gratification is important for this phase. Waiting is almost impossible for a two-year-old—*almost*. Just like your toddler needs to walk to strengthen his leg muscles, he needs to practice waiting to strengthen his patience and create a foundation for future financial responsibility. When he spots a toy at the check-out counter, it's okay to say, "Not this time."

You can exercise your toddler's ability by asking him to wait for short periods of time and rewarding his effort. Your toddler can wait (sixty seconds) for . . .
a drink.
a snack.
your undivided attention.

What are some other ways you can help your child practice patience?

....

....

....

....

....

....

....

GIVE THEM SOMEWHERE TO SERVE

Toddlers are notoriously self-centered. They love to talk about themselves, look at themselves, and do exclusively what they want. But that doesn't mean you can't begin to prompt them to share and help.

Your toddler can help the family. Even if the "help" isn't always helpful, encourage your toddler to do these things:

» Pick up his toys and put them away
» Clean up food that falls on the floor
» Bring you something you need
» Wipe up a spill—even if he mostly just spreads the liquid around

Your toddler can help others. For the most part, toddlers do not initiate serving others. Remember, their social skills are still developing.
The typical toddler will . . .
notice and wave to other children (19 – 24 months).
begin to share and take turns (26 – 30 months).
use polite language like "thank you" (26 – 30 months).

If you want your toddler to help and serve others, make serving a part of your family's life together. Here are a few suggestions:

» Set up a giving fund. Let your child be the one to physically give the money away. Tell your toddler how the money will help.
» Prompt your child to share or give away toys. Don't force him, but help your child see how giving can make someone else happy.
» Model the language of kindness and service by saying simple phrases around your home like, "please," "thank you," and "you go first."

What are some other ways your family models and practices serving others?

....

....

....

....

....

five

FUN/TIME
= CONNECTION

PLAY AND LAUGH TOGETHER MORE OFTEN

"Children need the freedom and time to play. Play is not a luxury. Play is a necessity."

KAY REDFIELD JAMISON

Play is the most common toddler activity. If your toddler isn't eating, sleeping, or crying, they are playing. For a toddler, play is both spontaneous and meaningful. It's the way they learn, discover, create, and have fun. Some sociologists actually attribute a person's social abilities to their play history as a child. In that sense, fun is one of the most important things you can give your toddler. And the fun you share with your child over time builds connection. In the phases to come, you will need a connection with your child that can only be built with fun.

That may sound like a lot of pressure to play. But most adults have really forgotten how. Even the most fun parents may struggle to know how to play with their toddler. Keep reading for three practical suggestions to have fun at One and Two.

TOYS

Your toddler will enjoy many toys. Just make sure to avoid things with cords and strings, plastic bags, sharp edges, small parts, or electricity.

TRUCKS, TRAINS, AND DOLLS
(12 months +)

SHAPE SORTERS
(12-18 months)

STACKING RINGS
(12-18 months)

PUSH TOYS
(12-18 months)

JUMBO CRAYONS
(15 months +)

A SOFT BALL FOR ROLLING AND THROWING
(16 months +)

PEG PUZZLES
(18-24 months)

BEAD MAZES
(18-24 months)

POUNDING BENCH
(19-24 months)

MEGA BLOCKS
(24-36 months)

RIDING/SCOOTING TOYS
(24-36 months)

PLAY-DOH
(24-36 months)

FINGER PAINT
(24-36 months)

PLAY KITCHEN
(24-36 months)

ALPHABET LETTERS
(24-36 months)

LEARN WHAT THEY LIKE

Your toddler likes toys. That's obvious. In fact, your toddler can turn just about anything into a toy—including everyday objects like a wooden spoon or saucepan lids. You don't have to turn your house into a museum of plastic noisemakers in order to entertain your child. But you should provide some safe, well-designed toys for your toddler to explore and interact with. Since your toddler is wired to play with anything she can find, make sure to keep her away from objects with cords and strings, plastic bags, sharp edges, small parts, or electricity.

LOOSEN UP

Before your toddler's third birthday, she isn't likely to do much playing with her peers. Sure, she may wave at a friend, give a hug, or play in the same space as her friends, but you are still her primary playmate. And she needs you to play with her for at least a few minutes every day. So loosen up. You have some serious playing to do.

» Go to the park
» Sing "Itsy Bitsy Spider"
» Blow bubbles
» Push a swing
» Roll a ball
» Do a silly dance
» Play airplane
» Play hide and seek (but don't hide or seek very well)

Your toddler needs prompts for interactive play. You may notice your younger toddler looking to you for prompts about what should happen next. Children under the age of two don't engage in solo acts of pretend play.[56] They also seldom direct imaginary play. But as your toddler gets older, you will be able to let her direct the game more and more. In the next phase, you are likely to find that your preschooler directs exactly what kind of game you should be playing and how you should play it.

Your toddler likes physical humor. When you set aside ten minutes to have fun with your toddler, get ready for some laughs. She may spontaneously turn a pancake into a "hat." Your toddler now understands and enjoys physical humor.[57]

That means you can make her laugh by . . .
acting forgetful or confused.
"accidentally" dropping something repeatedly.
pretending not to see what is in plain sight.
saying the wrong animal noise.
trying to use an everyday object for the wrong thing.

What are some other ways you've discovered you can use physical humor to make your toddler laugh?

....

....

....

....

Have someone record a video of that laugh. You will want to play it back again and again in years to come.

LOSE THE AGENDA

Play can raise your toddler's IQ, advance his athletic abilities, and improve social skills. But the best reason to play isn't because it's educational and purposeful. Sometimes toddlers (and people) need to have fun—just because it's fun.

Even if the fun seems silly.
Even if the fun lacks purpose.
Even if the fun doesn't lead to learning.
It's still worth it to JUST HAVE FUN.

When you play with your toddler, you show him that you are interested in him. You demonstrate that you like him. You let him know he is worth playing with. So each week, remember to set aside some time for fun.

six

TRIBES/TIME
= BELONGING

HELP THEM EXPERIENCE COMMUNITY

"'Why did you do all this for me?' he asked. 'I don't
deserve it. I've never done anything for you.' 'You have
been my friend,' replied Charlotte. 'That in itself is a
tremendous thing.'"

E.B. WHITE, *CHARLOTTE'S WEB*

"Tribe" may seem like a funny word. But a tribe is simply a group of
people connected by something in common. Your tribes are the people
you work with, the people you live with, and the people you hang out
with. Tribes convince us we are not alone, invisible, or unknown. As your
toddler grows up, part of your job as a parent will be to help him find his
place in multiple tribes. Nothing has the potential to give him a sense of
belonging like tribes over time. In this section are three ways to give your
toddler a tribe at One and Two.

CREATE APPEALING SPACES

Your toddler's first and most important tribe is your family. And just like every tribe has a place, your family has some shared spaces where you eat and sleep and play. Those spaces have the potential to connect you relationally, to communicate values, and to support the rhythm of your day.

Create designated spaces. Toddlers associate physical spaces with a particular routine, behavior, or expectation. So try to have a few predictable patterns.

How would you complete the following statements?

Every time my toddler is .... , we play together.

When my toddler is .... , she has independent playtime.

Every time my toddler is .... , he eats something.

Every time my toddler is .... , she is expected to sleep (and not play).

Of course you will have exceptions to the rule. Some days your toddler may nap in the car seat. Some days you may feed your toddler in your lap at the doctor's office. Some days you may accidentally both fall asleep on the play mat with trains all around you—it could happen.

Ideally, you will have some spaces in your home set up to meet three of your toddlers needs: eating, playing, and sleeping. Consider how to make these areas as functional as possible. Have some paper towels near the table. Take the light-up, musical toys out of the bedroom. Create spaces that communicate your expectations, and try to keep the exceptions the exception.

ESTABLISH SHARED TRADITIONS

Whether you are a single parent, an adoptive parent, a multi-generational family, a blended family, or a mixture of these, your family will be the most significant tribe to which your child will ever belong. Nothing has more influence on a child than family. And one of the things that makes your family your family are the traditions you share.

TRADITION:
a repeated pattern
of behavior

Some family traditions happen annually (like holidays and birthdays). We will talk more about how to celebrate those in the next section.

Some traditions happen within the rhythm of your week. They can be as simple as the way you . . .
pray with your toddler at bedtime.
greet your toddler with the same phrase each morning.
sing a familiar song as you change their diaper or give them a bath.

The traditions you establish in this phase may not remain the same over the next eighteen years. In fact, they probably shouldn't. But it's still important to have a few repeated behaviors that give your child a sense of security, draw you closer together as a family, and communicate the values of your tribe.

How would you complete the following statement?

In our family, we . . .

....

....

RECRUIT POSITIVE INFLUENCES

You've probably heard the saying, "It takes a village to raise a child." Even if we have no idea who said it first, it's absolutely true. A child has a better future when there are three to five adults who consistently show up and care for them.

Wait. Aren't *you* the most important influence in your toddler's life? Doesn't your toddler love you the most? Need you the most? Want to be around you the most? Yes. (Although, all of those won't always be true.)

Even though you are still the most important adult in your toddler's life, you aren't the only adult your toddler needs. It's never too early to begin to think about the community you want for your toddler as he grows.

In the One and Two Phase, you have more control over who influences your child than you will have in later phases. So be proactive.

Let your toddler . . .
spend time with extended family.
get to know a neighbor or close friend.
have a consistent hour each week in the church nursery.

Remember, while you have control over who will influence your toddler, you do not control everything those people will say and do around your toddler. It's still better for your toddler to have an afternoon with grandma —even if she feeds him marshmallows and chocolate pudding for lunch.

Name three to five adults who have influence with you and your toddler in this phase.

....

....

....

....

CELEB

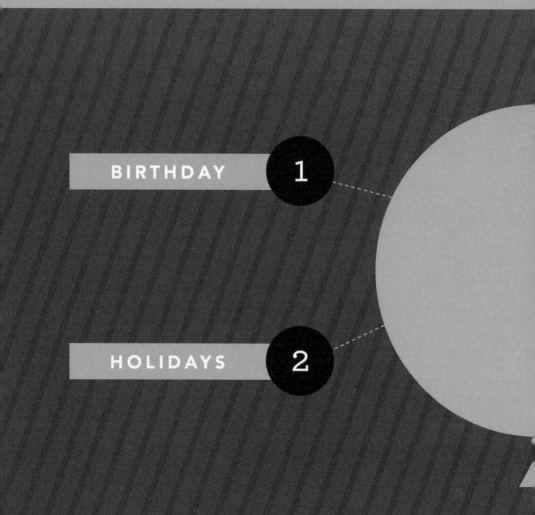

BIRTHDAY **1**

HOLIDAYS **2**

RATE

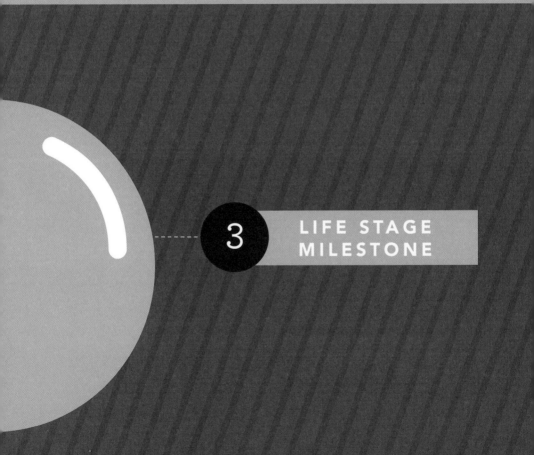

3 LIFE STAGE MILESTONE

Even though you have 884 weeks, all weeks aren't created equal.

Some moments only come around seasonally, annually, or once in a lifetime. And the way you celebrate those moments has a different kind of impact.

Over the next seventeen years with your child, some moments will create a shared experience, mark a significant milestone, or begin an annual tradition.

Their second birthday may be the last time you choose the theme for them. Their one- and two-year old Christmases may be the only time you do your shopping without a very specific wish list in

⏱ WEEKS

hand. And this might be the phase when you choose to celebrate the first chapter of life with a Baby Dedication. If you have created a countdown clock with marbles, you might consider including marbles that look different to represent these special moments.

This section won't tell you how to theme your child's second or third birthday party, but it will give you a few practical ideas for celebrating the big moments with your toddler in unique and memorable ways.

SO DON'T MISS THE **DISTINCTIVE** OPPORTUNITIES OF . . .

ONE
—AND—
TWO

one

BIRTHDAY

You have eighteen of these special days with your child while they're with you. So it's probably a good idea to start a few birthday traditions. Your traditions could be passed down from your own history, or you can steal from others on Facebook, Pinterest, or parenting blogs. Here are a few traditions to consider for the second and third birthday celebrations.

Birthday Breakfast: At two, your child has no idea it's their birthday. So start the day differently than any other. Wear a funny hat, have a special breakfast plate, put sprinkles on their oatmeal. Have fun coaching them to repeat, "I'm two," while holding up two chubby fingers.

Annual Birthday Playlist: Talk about the music you have enjoyed playing for your toddler this year. What songs did they sing and dance to most?

Create a playlist of favorite music from this year.

....

....

....

....

Record a Birthday Toast: At dinner or during cake, have each family member or guest share something that makes the birthday girl/boy special. Record a video of the toasts, or have guests write their toasts in letters for your child to read later.

Write your toast here:

....

....

....

....

....

....

....

....

Your child will have only two birthdays as a toddler. On the birthdays ahead, you will have more preschool friends to invite and more specific gift requests to fulfill. For now, enjoy inviting your friends and family. That's okay—they're the ones helping you raise your silly, bright, and wonderfully perfect two-year-old.

And as for presents, consider this. Toddlers are not very good at sharing— just yet. Many parents find, in this phase, it's better to wait until the guests leave to open presents. Instead of opening new toys in front of a room full of two-year-olds, take photos of your child opening gifts and text quick "thank-you" pictures to the gift givers. During the party, your toddler will probably be too excited about the cake to mind waiting on presents, and you are far more likely to avoid an unfortunate meltdown situation.

two

HOLIDAYS

Every holiday with a toddler is a brand-new opportunity for panic. What will they wear? Will they refuse to nap at Grandma's house? It's impossible to avoid holiday stress completely. But the holidays with your one- and two-year-old can also be uniquely delightful. Here are a few ideas to help you capture the joy of these special moments:

EASTER
Your toddler understands resurrection about as well as he hunts for Easter eggs.[58] "Hide" the eggs low, let him hunt before any big kids join, and emphasize how much Jesus loves him. Go to church. Hug your toddler and say, *"On Easter, we are happy because Jesus loves us!"*

HALLOWEEN
Your two-year-old may be thrilled by the chance to dress up—or they may decide that minion costume is too itchy, too tight, or too yellow. Either way, take a picture. Celebrate at a community festival. Let your toddler help you pass out some candy.

THANKSGIVING
This is a chance to pawn off your child on adoring relatives *and* eat a delicious meal—if someone else cooks it. Use this season to talk about things you are thankful for. Say prayers of thanks together. It can be as simple as, "Jesus, thank You for Mommy. (*Pause.*) Thank You for Daddy. (*Pause.*) Thank You for loving us. (*Pause.*)"

CHRISTMAS

Christmas is one of the best holidays to have a few family traditions. Whether your traditions remain constant or change with the phases, go ahead and try a few this year to embrace the faith, joy, and energy your toddler will bring to Christmas.

Four Gift Ideas: Your toddler probably doesn't have a long wish list—but you might. Ask doting friends and relatives to help by choosing gifts that fit into one of four categories: something they want, something they need, something to wear, something to read.

Nativity Story Time: If you have a nativity in your home, show your toddler the different pieces as you set up the scene. Talk about the characters and tell the story as you put the pieces in place.

Christmas Traditions: Continue or establish other traditions like:

» New pajamas on Christmas Eve
» A keepsake ornament for the tree
» A visit to Santa (even if they cry when you hand them to the bearded stranger)
» A drive through the sparkling lights
» A special Christmas book to read before bed

OTHER PARTY DAYS

Truly, you don't need an excuse to party with your child! When your toddler needs to burn off some extra energy, pick a holiday and go for it. Try one of these ideas or take to the Internet for a national holiday every month of the year! (We bet your toddler is already celebrating No Pants Day on May 6.)

Puppy Day............................ March 23
Dance Like a Chicken Day ... May 14
Cousins Day .... July 24
Eat Outside Day .... August 31
Make a Hat Day.................... September 15

three

LIFE STAGE MILESTONE

LIFE STAGE MILESTONE:
an event that marks and celebrates a significant moment or change in a person's story

Unlike other celebrations, life stage milestones happen only once in a person's life. They should never be celebrated alone. Maybe that's because it's hard to karaoke without an audience, or because most cakes aren't sold by the slice. Or maybe it's because these moments have a unique potential to help frame a kid's identity and mark their position in the community.

When you celebrate a life stage milestone, you acknowledge something significant has happened. You gather with the people who know you best. You tell stories that celebrate your history, clarify your present, and imagine your future. These are powerful moments to define or reinforce something about who your child is and who they are becoming.

Simply put:

» A milestone marks a change in my story and our story.
» A milestone celebrates a change in who I am and who we are.

BEGINNING: CELEBRATING THE FIRST CHAPTER OF LIFE

The first years of your child's life are a time for you to identify your community, surround yourself with support, and imagine what you want to be true for your child's future. You may call the celebration by any number of names. In its simplest form, a Baby Dedication is a moment in time when you publicly commit to parenting with the future faith of your child in mind.

When you celebrate a Baby Dedication, you create a moment outside the day-to-day chaos to imagine the life you want for your toddler in the years to come. You move outside the immediate issues at hand and prioritize the things that matter most.

You may have already dedicated your child, but if you haven't, it's definitely not too late to do it now. Here are a few ideas that could help you celebrate this once-in-a-lifetime moment.

INVITE SIGNIFICANT PEOPLE

Use this time to celebrate the ways other people have invested in your own life. Let them know you will need them to help you parent this child. Invite them into the process because there will come a day in the not-so-distant future when you will no longer be enough, and the other adults in your child's life will take on a more significant role.

Make a list of people who have invested in your life who you want to invite to your Baby Dedication.

....

....

....

....

....

CLARIFY WHAT MATTERS

As you imagine the end, who do you want your child to become? If you had to prioritize three to five characteristics you hope are true for your child in the future, what would they be? Write down these characteristics. This list is your ultimate destination. It will help you navigate big decisions in the future. Share these characteristics with those you invite to your child's Baby Dedication. It will help them better support you and your child in the years to come.

What are three to five characteristics you hope will be true about your child in the future?

....

....

....

....

....

....

....

....

....

....

....

....

....

CREATE A PHYSICAL REMINDER

You may want to give a gift, like a first storybook Bible, to commemorate the moment. You may choose to plant a tree. You could take a picture, write down who came and what they said, and write a letter for your child to open on a significant birthday or at graduation. There are a hundred ways to mark the significance of this moment. The way you commemorate it is entirely up to you.

What's one way to commemorate your Baby Dedication?

....

....

....

....

....

....

Look for more ideas on Baby Dedication and how to clarify what matters on TheParentcue.com.

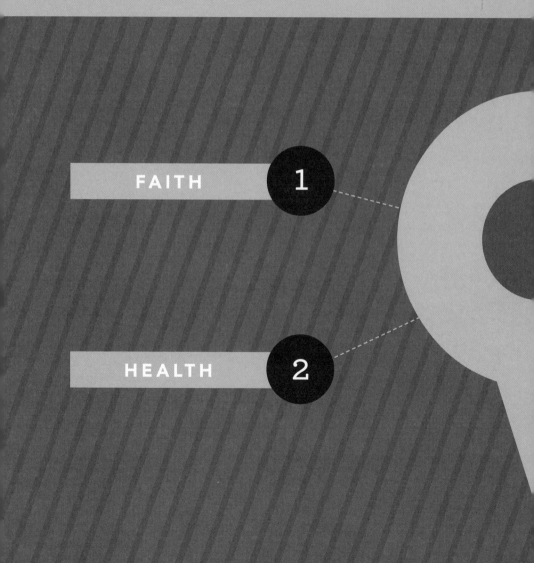

NAVI

<u>THE</u> **CRITICAL ISSUES**

FAITH   **1**

HEALTH   **2**

GATE

3   SEX

4   TECHNOLOGY

Over the next 884 weeks, you will face many parenting dilemmas. Should your child wear the hand-me-down jumper from Aunt Paula on picture day? Will you use Pampers Easy-Ups® or Huggies Pull-Ups® for training pants? But there will be seemingly more subtle parenting issues that have a greater impact on your child's future.

In fact, there are at least four critical issues that are common for every phase: FAITH, HEALTH, SEX, and TECHNOLOGY. They seem subtle now, but in the phases ahead these critical issues will intensify. And the way you navigate these issues during the next 104 weeks will impact the 780 weeks that follow.

WEEKS

That's why it's a good thing you've picked up this book. Every answer you will ever need for successfully parenting through faith, health, sex, and technology can be found in the next twenty-eight pages.

Okay. Maybe not. But this next section is an overview with a few practical steps to help you begin navigating these critical issues in a way that is both phase-specific and future-oriented.

SO DON'T MISS THE FUTURE IMPLICATIONS OF . . .

ONE
— AND —
TWO

//

IMAGINE
THE END

//

There are a host of things you will navigate over the next several years like managing wardrobes, rating movies, maybe even refereeing sibling rivalries. We just picked FAITH, HEALTH, SEX, and TECHNOLOGY because after countless conversations with teachers, Starbucks® managers, physicians, therapists, and parole officers, these four issues surfaced more than most.

The best parenting strategy for navigating these four critical issues at every phase is to imagine the end. "Imagining the end" means you consider now the things you want to be true in your child's life later—when you help them move into a dorm room or first apartment. It means you identify the end goal, and then rewind your parenting strategy and begin thinking in terms of specific steps that can be applied at every phase.

For example . . .
If you want your child to graduate from high school,
    then enroll them in the first grade.
If you want your child to have positive friendships,
    then give them opportunities to play with peers.
If you want your child to be a professional athlete,
    then make sure they're born with some natural talent.

When you imagine the end, you begin by identifying the goal. On the next page are four goals that you can customize to reflect what you would like to see happen in the life of your son or daughter. Just remember, keeping your goals in mind will help you stay focused, prioritize your efforts, and maintain perspective.

4 END GOALS

AUTHENTIC FAITH

TRUSTING JESUS IN A WAY THAT TRANSFORMS HOW I LOVE GOD, MYSELF, AND THE REST OF THE WORLD

HEALTHY HABITS

LEARNING TO STRENGTHEN MY BODY THROUGH EXERCISE, NUTRITION, AND SELF-ADVOCACY

SEXUAL INTEGRITY

GUARDING MY POTENTIAL FOR INTIMACY THROUGH APPROPRIATE BOUNDARIES AND MUTUAL RESPECT

TECHNOLOGICAL RESPONSIBILITY

LEVERAGING THE POTENTIAL OF ONLINE EXPERIENCES TO ENHANCE MY OFFLINE COMMUNITY AND SUCCESS

CREATE A RHYTHM

Before we talk about phase-specific strategies to help you navigate FAITH, HEALTH, SEX, and TECHNOLOGY, consider this:

The most significant things you will give your son or daughter are the things you give them over time. That's what can trick you as a parent. In the One and Two Phase, it might seem as if nothing significant is happening. But what you do every week adds up to a collection of weeks. The day-to-day moments matter more than you realize.

One of the simplest and most effective strategies for navigating critical issues at every phase is to create a rhythm to your week. In other words, use the time you already have to accomplish what you know you need to do.

In Deuteronomy 6:7, Moses gives instructions to the nation of Israel on how they could pass their faith on to the next generation:

Impress them on your children. Talk about them when you sit at home and when you walk along the road, when you lie down and when you get up.

Your strategy should be similar. The best way to help your child navigate faith, health, sex, and technology is to use the everyday routine that comes with caring for your toddler.

 # 4 FAMILY TIMES

MORNING TIME

SET THE MOOD FOR THE DAY

Smile and greet them with words of love.

DRIVE TIME

REINFORCE SIMPLE IDEAS

Talk to your toddler and play music as you go.

BATH TIME

WIND DOWN TOGETHER

Provide comfort as the day draws to a close.

CUDDLE TIME

BE PERSONAL

Spend one-on-one time that communicates love and affection.

one

FAITH
BY: REGGIE JOINER

IMAGINE THE END:
AUTHENTIC FAITH

Trusting Jesus in a way that transforms
how I love God, myself, and the rest of the world

Your child is created in the image of God. Maybe that sounds obvious, or maybe it's hard to believe on some days. But stop and think about that for a moment. It's what makes authentic faith possible for your child.

Your chubby-cheeked, runny-nosed, toddling child is made in God's image. That means she actually has a divine capacity to reason, to care, and to believe. She is drawn to the One who created her in His image.

Maybe that's why your toddler sees the world with such wonder:
every flower
every rock
every light-up toy

There is simply no other phase of life when your child will have the kind of wonder, amazement, and delight they possess as a toddler. They will gaze open-mouthed, wide-eyed at a plastic dump truck.

But you can tap into your toddler's natural sense of wonder as you introduce her to the Creator of all things (even the One who makes plastic dump trucks). In the One and Two Phase, you can influence how your toddler sees God when you do one thing.

IN THE ONE AND TWO PHASE

You will incite
WONDER.

When you incite wonder in the heart of a preschooler, you help them see that the world is full of amazing things because it was created by an amazing God. You let them know they have the ability to do good because they were created by a good Creator.

As you incite wonder in the heart of your toddler, remember this. You and other caring adults will become your child's first impression of God. That's why everything you do is in the context of embracing his physical needs. When you take your toddler to the potty, get him a snack, and respond to his call, your are giving him an early impression of love and care. And practically speaking, the way you embrace his needs will give you the ability to incite wonder so that your toddler can . . .

KNOW GOD'S LOVE
& MEET GOD'S FAMILY

Stated another way, in the One and Two Phase your job is simple—to love your toddler like God loves you and to introduce him to people who reflect God's love. On the next page are five specific things you can do in the rhythm of your week to incite a toddler's sense of wonder for their Creator.

PRAY FOR THEM WHILE YOU ARE WITH THEM

There is something special about praying for a child while you are with them. They may not understand all of your words, but they can sense your attitude toward God. And in this phase, they may begin imitating what they see you do.

PLAY AND SING FAITH SONGS

Toddlers respond to music. Just think about all the dancing toddler videos on YouTube. There's something in those chubby thighs that wants to move and shake when they hear the rhythm. A simple tune like "Jesus Loves Me" can delight a toddler while communicating truth. So sing or play songs that remind your family about God's love.

CONNECT WITH A FAITH COMMUNITY

In this phase there will be good days and bad days. Even though getting your toddler dressed, fed, redressed, changed, and dressed again can be a little bit of a challenge, it's worth it. Find a church where you feel welcome, known, and connected. Your toddler needs a faith community to show her that God is bigger than just her family. And you need a faith community to remind you that you're not in this alone.

READ BIBLE STORIES

Your toddler isn't ready for a full-text Bible just yet. She might even treat books in general with a little irreverence. If left alone, there's a chance she will even chew on or tear out the pages. But you can introduce her to the idea that the Bible is a book, and you can read stories that capture her imagination about God. Read Bible storybooks with stories about Creation, Christmas, and Easter.

REPEAT BASIC TRUTHS

Your toddler is learning to speak two- and three-word sentences—most of them in reference to something she wants or doesn't want. She probably won't memorize many memory verses this year. But it's not too early for your toddler to grasp some basic faith concepts. Keep it simple, use repetition, and focus on what matters most. We think there are at least three basic truths worth repeating regularly to your toddler.

* For more ideas on how to leverage time and faith activities every week, check out the Parent CUE app on Android or iPhone.

3 BASIC TRUTHS

1 GOD MADE ME

2 GOD LOVES ME

3 JESUS WANTS TO BE MY FRIEND FOREVER

AUTHENTIC FAITH

Incite
WONDER

Pray for them
And pray aloud while you are with them.

Sing faith songs
Start with "Jesus Loves Me."

Connect with a faith community
Find one that supports both you and your child.

Read Bible stories
Select stories that capture their imagination about God.

ZERO
to ONE

ONE
& TWO

EMBRACE

Trusting Jesus in a way that transforms how I love God, myself, and the rest of the world

→

SO THEY WILL . . .
KNOW GOD'S LOVE
& MEET GOD'S FAMILY

Repeat basic truths
Say things like:
"God made me."
"God loves me."
"Jesus wants to be my friend forever."

Encourage them to pray
Pray aloud while you are together.

Prompt them to share and help

Answer faith questions

THREE
& FOUR

THEIR PHYSICAL NEEDS

two

HEALTH
BY: DR. JEAN SUMNER

IMAGINE THE END:
HEALTHY HABITS

Learning to strengthen my body through
exercise, nutrition, and self-advocacy

Your toddler is a one of a kind, remarkable human. Remember that. In this
phase, many parents fall into a comparison trap. They ask questions like,

"My niece seems to talk non-stop, is that normal? My daughter still only
 says two words at a time."

"My two-year-old isn't eating as much as last year. Is that okay?"

"Our neighbor has a son who knocks a baseball over the fence, should my
 son be doing that?"

Fear can creep in fast when you compare your child to his siblings, his
peers, or even his last-year-self. Fear is a natural part of parenting. It
comes with loving someone so much. But fear won't help your child's
health. So first, take a deep breath and relax.

Your child was made in the image of God with a remarkable ability to grow and develop. His growth doesn't depend on you getting everything right. In many ways, his growth will happen in spite of you.

But that doesn't mean your toddler doesn't need you. No one knows your toddler better than you, so you will likely be the first to notice when something changes. There are many reasons to call your pediatrician, such as a fever over 103 degrees, a fever that lasts longer than three days, or if your toddler is lethargic. But the greatest rule to live by is to trust your instincts. If you are concerned about your child's health, call your pediatrician. In this phase, your toddler cannot always communicate when something is wrong. So when you notice a change, and you communicate with your doctor, you can be your child's greatest advocate.

As a parent, the greatest thing you can do for your child's health may not seem all that remarkable. Beyond fighting illness, this is the phase when you will lay a foundation for a lifetime of healthy habits.

IN THE ONE AND TWO PHASE

You will
ESTABLISH
basic nutrition.

Basic nutrition may seem . . . too basic. But remember all the ways your toddler is changing. There's an unbelievable amount of growth that happens in this phase, and the best way to support all of that growth is to help your toddler . . .

HAVE CONSISTENT HEALTHCARE
& ENJOY A VARIETY OF FOODS

By giving your toddler these basics, you give him not only what his growing body needs right now, but also what he needs in order to have healthy habits in the future. The next page lists six practical ways to establish basic nutrition in the "I can do it" phase.

PRIORITIZE WELL VISITS

No one has more potential to partner with you to influence your child's health over the next 884 weeks than your pediatrician. Make sure you have a doctor you trust. You need a health professional who makes you feel comfortable enough that you can bring up the things that concern you—like the half-chewed gum your child found on the sidewalk and tasted last week. After all, your relationship with your pediatrician requires mutual respect and honesty. When you go to your well visits at 12, 15, 18, and 24 months, try to see the same pediatrician so you can build history together. The better your pediatrician knows your child, the more helpful they can be in treating your child.

CREATE A FILE FOR HEALTH RECORDS

Even in a digital world where your doctor keeps an online account of your visits, it's best for you to keep your own medical records on file. These records create a history that will help you and your child advocate for the best health care in the years to come. Consider extending these records to include details about your child's biological medical history, whether that is your own family or the medical history of a birth mother and father. If you want to trace the medical history of your own family, ask for help from grandparents. They like to give gifts to their grandkids. And their knowledge about your child's genetic line may be worth considerably more than an Elmo doll or Winnie the Pooh stickers in the future.

PLAY OUTSIDE

Of course exercise is important. But right now, in the toddler phase, you probably aren't enlisting them in a heavy weight-lifting regime—because you shouldn't. Your toddler's developing bones need only to lift the weight of their growing body. The best exercise for your toddler is the exercise they get while playing. Some of that will happen naturally inside as they climb on your sofa, your table, and your pantry shelves trying to reach their favorite snack. But when the weather is sunny, try to let your toddler have some outside playtime as well. Take them to the park and let them run outside, for your sanity as well as theirs. The combination of fresh air and vitamin D will strengthen their body, and if you're lucky, it will help them take a better nap later.

FIGHT FOR REST

Speaking of naps, your toddler needs between 11-14 hours of sleep per day. Around 18 months, your toddler may achieve this rest with one afternoon nap in addition to their nighttime sleep. Bedtime battles are common at this age, especially if you have transitioned your toddler out of their crib. The best way to help your toddler get rest is to have a consistent bedtime routine, a familiar calm environment at night, and a security object like a blanket or teddy bear for nighttime comfort.

LIMIT SUGARY TREATS

You will never avoid sugar altogether—at least not with grandma around. And that's not to mention that toddlers will do anything for a Skittle. The temptation to reward good behavior with treats is just too great. But toddlers also like stickers. Look for ways to keep the sugar to a minimum so your toddler can develop a taste for food groups that don't come with plastic wrappers.

OFFER HEALTHY SNACKS

Toddlers are grazers. Their busy little bodies like to keep moving, and they would rather play and snack than sit still for a full meal. Snacks between meals are okay, as long as the snack isn't always french fries or a bag of cheese puffs. The best way to provide healthy nutrition for your toddler is to keep healthy snack options on hand. Try yogurt, fruit, raw vegetables like carrots, or baked chips. Your toddler still needs plenty of calcium, so let them drink milk. And offer water more often than juice.

MINIMIZE GERMS

Oh, the runny noses. The dirty security blanket. The sticky hands. This phase comes with germs, germs, and more germs. You will never eliminate all the germs. But you should begin some routines now that will lay a foundation for personal hygiene. Brush your toddler's teeth twice a day. If your child is resistant, try singing a fun song or make a game out of tooth-brushing time to help make it more enjoyable and more effective. Help your toddler wash their hands regularly, especially after using the potty. And remember, hand sanitizer doesn't take the place of soap and water.

HEALTHY HABITS

ESTABLISH
basic nutrition

Begin a relationship with a pediatrician

Prioritize well visits
Go to the pediatrician the first week after your baby is born, then at 1, 2, 4, 6, 9, and 12 months.

Create a file for storing health records

Give the best nutrients possible
Breastfeeding is recommended for the first twelve months.

Prioritize well visits
Go at 12, 15, 18, and 24 months.

Let them play outside and get rest

Limit sugary treats
Toddlers will do anything for a Skittle, but they also like stickers.

ZERO to ONE

ONE & TWO

EMBRACE

Learning to strengthen my
body through exercise, nutrition,
and self-advocacy

SO THEY WILL . . .
HAVE CONSISTENT HEALTHCARE
& EXPERIENCE A VARIETY OF FOOD

Offer healthy snacks

Minimize germs
Brush teeth 2x
a day, and wash
hands regularly
(hand sanitizer
isn't soap).

Have an annual visit to the pediatrician

Keep trying healthy foods
Say things like: "It's
okay if you don't
like it today. You
might like it later."

Cook together

Talk about where food comes from

Encourage sports for fun
Four-year-olds
don't need to
be drafted into
a competitive
league.

THREE
& FOUR

THEIR PHYSICAL NEEDS

three

SEX

BY: DR. JIM BURNS

IMAGINE THE END:
SEXUAL INTEGRITY

Guarding my potential for intimacy through
appropriate boundaries and mutual respect

If you want to raise your child to have sexual integrity one day, it begins
with an understanding that we have all been made in the image of God.

When a child believes they have been made in the image of God, and
when they see others as made in the image of God as well, it profoundly
affects their relationships:

It changes the way they feel about their own body.
It changes their view of how they should treat other people.
It changes the way they navigate their sexuality.

It may seem like it's too early to talk about things like sexuality. But in fact,
research shows that having conversations with children, beginning when
they are very young, delays the age at which they begin having sex and

makes it less likely that they will engage in risky sexual behaviors.[59] That means *now* is the perfect time to begin the conversation.

This is a phase characterized by:

» Rapid physical growth
» Curiosity about their body
» No inhibitions around nudity

One- and two-year-olds are also notorious for taking their clothes off (more often than keeping them on), exploring their own bodies (in public as well as private), and rubbing their private parts (often to the horror of their parents).

Sexuality is as much a part of who we are as our own elbow. It's with us from the beginning. So even though you may not be having "The Talk" with your two-year-old, you do have a role to play in navigating this critical issue.

IN THE ONE AND TWO PHASE

You will
INTRODUCE
them to their body.

As you introduce your child to the body God made for them, you let them know their body is a good and acceptable thing. You begin very early in life helping your child know they have been well-made because they were made by and made in the image of a good Creator.

In this phase you are beginning a conversation that will continue to develop in the phases to come. For now, you will help them . . .

**DISCOVER THEIR BODY
& DEFINE PRIVACY**

So let's keep it simple. Here are four things you can do now that will help lay a foundation for the many talks to come.

START WITH THE BASICS

Tell your child "God made you." When it makes sense to do so, use specific examples like, "God made your beautiful eyes." And, "God made your strong legs."

NAME BODY PARTS

Your toddler is learning words for everything they see. As you bathe and change your toddler, give her words for her body parts. Sing "Head, Shoulders, Knees and Toes." Don't be afraid to also say, "That's your vagina/penis." Your toddler may need to know the words for their body parts if they need to explain when something hurts or if something made them uncomfortable. Giving your toddler the words to name her body also communicates that you are okay with their body. If it makes you uncomfortable to say the words now, consider this practice for the conversations you have ahead of you. And remember, your toddler is sensitive to shame. So whatever you do, don't say, "Look at your tiny little wee-wee."

ACKNOWLEDGE DIFFERENCES

Toddlers discover their world by putting things into categories. They want to know which things are edible and which things are not. They want to know which things light up and make music and which things don't. They will probably also begin to notice that some people are "boys like me" or "girls like me," and some are not. As they notice differences, you may find yourself saying things like, "Boys grow up to be men like Daddy or Uncle Frank."

DEFINE PRIVACY

As you begin potty training, you will also begin privacy training. It may take a few years for your toddler to really grasp the concept, but begin now by saying things like, "Private parts are meant to be private." If you have an especially touchy toddler, be careful not to shame him by exclaiming, "Why do you keep touching your privates?!" Instead redirect his attention. Later, when the moment has passed, remind him in a calm voice, "We don't touch our private places in public."

"If you start the conversation with your child now, you will have many opportunities to expand the conversation in an age-appropriate manner as they grow and mature. You will have a foundation to build on as the years go by."

MARY FLO RIDLEY

SEXUAL INTEGRITY

INTRODUCE
them to their body

Start with the basics
Say things like: "God made your strong legs."

Name body parts
Use the real names for private parts— *you know them.*

Acknowledge differences
Say things like: "Boys grow up to be men like Daddy or Uncle Frank."

Define privacy
Say things like: "Private parts are meant to be private."

ZERO to ONE

ONE & TWO

EMBRACE

Guarding my potential for intimacy through appropriate boundaries and mutual respect

Coach privacy
Say things like:
"Sometimes it's polite to look away."

Answer simple questions
Say things like:"Babies grow inside of their mama until it's time to be born."

Affirm a positive view of their growing body
Say things like:
"I love watching you grow."

THREE
& FOUR

THEIR PHYSICAL NEEDS

four

TECHNOLOGY
BY: JON ACUFF

IMAGINE THE END:
TECHNOLOGICAL RESPONSIBILITY

Leveraging the potential of online experiences to
enhance my offline community and success

Living with a toddler is like inviting a small hurricane inside your house.
It's the perfect climate for keeping technology safe, right? Wrong. Let's
be honest. In this phase you are mostly trying to protect your technology
from your kid.

There are some phases ahead when you will be more concerned with
keeping your kid safe from technology. And as strange as it may seem,
the road to get there starts here. On the one hand, you can't imagine the
end for technology, because who can predict what gear and gadgets we'll
have in five to ten years? On the other hand, you can create a goal and
a strategy that will result in the kind of technological freedom that will
enhance, rather than limit, your child's future.

The key to technological responsibility is the ability to see yourself and everyone else as created in the image of God.

Through that lens, technology can become a vehicle to develop a child's sense of wonder, their learning, their community, and even their self-image. Technology can increase a kid's potential to do good and their ability to discover a purpose.

That may seem like a pretty big goal when your child pronounces iPad as "high pad." But even in this phase, you play a role in their technological engagement.

| IN THE ONE AND TWO PHASE | You will ENJOY the advantages. |

It's the easiest role you've had in your life. Parenting a toddler is hard work, but guess what? Technology has some incredible benefits. Of course, enjoying the advantages doesn't mean just turning on a video and letting the screen buy you an extra hour of quiet. That's probably not the best early foundation for future technological responsibility. Right now you are helping your toddler . . .

EXPERIENCE BOUNDARIES
& HAVE POSITIVE EXPOSURE

In other words, the best way to help your toddler grow up with technological responsibility in the future is for you to enjoy the advantages of technology responsibly now. So, what does this mean practically? On the next page are four ideas to help you enjoy the advantages of technology responsibly with your toddler.

CAPTURE THE MOMENTS

Capture as many moments as you can, but if you find yourself absent from the moment because you're picking the perfect filter to capture it, put the phone down and be present. It's easy to get stuck watching kids develop through six-inch screens instead of the 360-degree eyes you already have. No matter how great technology gets, the memory you make will always have higher resolution.

PURCHASE THE PROTECTION PLAN

Keep Sharpies® and your tablet in very different parts of the house. Put your laptop on higher shelves than you think is necessary. It's hard to get Play-Doh® out of the headset jack. If you remember nothing else, this one paragraph will have made this book worth roughly fifty times what you paid for it.

LIMIT THEIR SCREEN TIME

The American Academy of Pediatrics recommends zero screen time before a kid's second birthday.[60] Zero isn't very much. It's just what doctors and developmental experts say is the ideal—kind of like getting three servings of vegetables a day. But even with limited screen time, it's easy to let the minutes—or hours—sneak up when you aren't looking. Keep your finger on the pulse, or in this case, the play button for your toddler. Remember, in this phase, they learn far better from people than screens.

AVOID HEADPHONES

A toddler's ears are more sensitive than adults—just take your toddler to watch a fireworks display and see what happens. But the toddler who cries when fireworks hurt their ears may not have the same reaction when it comes to listening to their favorite song at full volume. Over time, exposure to loud noise can lead to hearing loss, and not just the selective hearing that will inevitably kick in when you ask your two-year-old to, "Stop jumping next to the cat's face."

"The pixel quality on a cardboard box is horrible but it still might be your toddler's favorite toy. That's okay. Your toddler may learn less with the expensive gadget than he can from the box it came in."

JON ACUFF

TECHNOLOGICAL RESPONSIBILITY

ENJOY
the advantages

Use the tools, but don't be used by them
If you forgot to record a diaper change in an app, it still happened.

Connect to other adults
Remember you're not alone.

Make sure you don't miss a real moment to capture a digital one

Purchase the protection plan
It's hard to get Play-Doh® out of the headset jack.

Limit their screen time

ZERO
to ONE

ONE
& TWO

EMBRACE

Leveraging the potential of online experiences to enhance my offline community and success

SO THEY WILL . . .
EXPERIENCE BOUNDARIES & HAVE POSITIVE EXPOSURE

→

Turn off in-app purchasing
Toddler fingers are great at online shopping.

Use technology for learning
Every digital device can be a classroom.

Play online games together

Have some screen-free zones and screen-free times at home

THREE & FOUR

THEIR PHYSICAL NEEDS

NAVIGATING A CRISIS

CRISIS:
A real or perceived threat
to your child

Earlier in this book we talked about the predictable crisis that most toddlers feel due to their changing abilities. This section is about navigating unpredictable crisis. The kind that sneaks up on you. The kind that may be hard to recognize. The kind that most parents' sheltering instinct makes them hope their child never experiences.

Navigating crisis is unlike navigating technology or health. You won't parent through it at every phase. Instead, you will parent your child through a crisis—when it happens.

We are including this guide in case your child experiences a crisis as a one- and two-year-old. Because, like so many other things, the way you recognize and respond to your child's crisis will look different at every phase.

RECOGNIZING A TODDLER IN CRISIS

It's easy to miss that your child might be in crisis at any stage, especially during the early years. Your toddler probably won't clue you in with sophisticated verbal cues:

"Mom, I'm really having a hard time with this move . . . "
"I think I'm not sleeping well ever since Grandma passed away . . . "

But just because your toddler isn't talking about it, doesn't mean they are unaffected. In fact, toddlers can be affected by anything that would affect an adult: death, loss of a job, relocation, divorce, abuse, even a national crisis. If you are concerned your toddler may be having a hard time, here are three things to ask yourself:

1 **Are they regressing?**
Especially with younger toddlers, regression is your first clue that something may be troubling them. During a crisis, toddlers will often take control of their own world by regressing in physical and mental abilities. Look at regressions in potty training, verbal skills, motor development, or behavior as an indicator of crisis.

2 **How are they playing?**
Toddlers may act out what they are trying to process. Watch as your toddler plays with toys. Notice how he manipulates the toys to interact and treat each other. If the toys seem especially angry or hurt, consider whether there might be a real source for those emotions.

3 **What are they drawing?**
Similar to play, as your toddler gets older, he may also draw what he is processing. His art is like a window into his mind. It may be hard to interpret the scribbles, so make it a habit to ask your toddler about his drawings. You may discover the drawing is a representation of something that bothered him.

RESPONDING TO A TODDLER IN CRISIS

There's no one solution to restoring balance in your toddler's world. But here are a few practical ideas for navigating through the crisis together:

Reestablish some routine. Toddlers thrive when they have a level of predictability, but a crisis often means a change to the normal routine.

» Talk about the changes together.
» Remind them of what hasn't changed.
» Establish new expectations.
» Create a new rhythm that will reestablish some routine.

Play with them. If you notice a change in your child's play, join him on the floor. Pick up a toy and join in the play. Use the toy as a way to have a non-threatening conversation. Spending thirty minutes of focused one-on-one play with your child may be one of the best ways to establish a connection and help him navigate crisis.

Make music. Music is healing. It's multi-sensory, non-threatening, structured, personalized, fun, and accessible. If you are processing crisis, take time to just play music together. It won't help you talk through your problems, but it will help you and your toddler feel better.

Respect their boundaries. Physical affection is a natural response to someone who is hurting, and there are many reasons you should give your toddler frequent hugs and kisses. But a toddler in crisis may be feeling out of control, so it's important to respect their boundaries. Consider asking, "Would you like for me to hold you?" "Do you want a hug?" In asking these questions, you offer them control of their body and their world. You may find your toddler needs a safe space alone to process his emotions before he is ready for your physical affection.

Take care of yourself. It's hard to save someone when you are drowning. When your preschooler is in crisis, it may mean you have experienced a crisis as well. Seek care. Find community. Take some personal time. Prioritizing your own physical and mental health is never selfish. It may be the best thing you can do for your child.

Get outside help. There may be times when you aren't the only one your child needs in order to navigate crisis. Trust your gut. If you suspect you may need outside help, get it. For a guideline on when to get help, consider these four things:

» If your toddler is being hurt by someone
» If your toddler is hurting others
» If your toddler is hurting themselves
» If you are hurting and not currently in a place emotionally or mentally where you can provide rational support

WHAT'S COMING UP

ONE OF THE JOYS OF PARENTING IS THE MANY SURPRISES THAT GREET YOU AROUND EVERY CORNER.

WE CAN'T PREPARE YOU FOR ALL THE JOYS THAT AWAIT YOU IN THE NEXT PHASE, BUT WE CAN GIVE YOU A GLIMPSE OF A FEW THINGS THAT MIGHT HELP YOU ANTICIPATE WHAT'S COMING.

» MEETING YOUR CHILD'S IMAGINARY FRIEND

» PLAYING YOUR FIRST BOARD GAME TOGETHER

» TEACHING YOUR CHILD TO RIDE A TRICYCLE

» GOING TO SEE A MOVIE IN A MOVIE THEATER

» READING A BOOK WITH A PLOT YOU ACTUALLY ENJOY

» CHECKING UNDER THE BED FOR MONSTERS

» DISCOVERING YOUR PRESCHOOLER NOW "HATES" ALL FOOD

» DRESS UP/IMAGINARY PLAY

» COVERING YOUR FRIDGE WITH PRICELESS ART

» YOUR PRESCHOOLER DRESSING HERSELF—IN THE OUTFIT SHE CHOSE

» EVEN WORSE TEMPER TANTRUMS

» GOING TO THEIR FIRST DENTIST APPOINTMENT

» IMPROVING YOUR NEGOTIATING SKILLS EVERY NIGHT AROUND BEDTIME

» LAUGHING. LOTS OF LAUGHING.

NEXT

IN ONLY

52

WEEKS

THE

"I CAN DO IT"

PHASE WILL BEGIN TO FADE INTO THE PAST.

YOU WILL BEGIN TO DISCOVER A NEW PHASE WITH A WHOLE NEW SET OF

PRESENT REALITIES

DISTINCTIVE OPPORTUNITIES

AND

FUTURE IMPLICATIONS

SO, MAKE THE MOST OF THIS PRESENT PHASE BECAUSE BEFORE YOU KNOW IT, YOU WILL FIND YOURSELF FACING A NEW PHASE.

IN NOT SO MANY WEEKS YOU MAY DISCOVER YOU ARE LIVING WITH A CURIOUS PRESCHOOLER WHO REALLY WANTS TO KNOW,

"WHY?"

THREE
AND FOUR

THE PHASE WHEN ANYTHING CAN
BE IMAGINED, EVERYTHING CAN
BE A GAME, AND ONE CURIOUS
PRESCHOOLER WANTS TO KNOW,
"WHY?"

IMAGINATION IS REALITY.

Your preschooler might suddenly become a self-proclaimed princess, pirate, or superhero. Your bedroom might turn out to be a train station, a castle, or both. But imagination may also turn scary. Fear may set in when at any given moment, a monster can show up in the hallway, a snake can be under the bed, or a dragon can walk through the living room.

EVERYTHING CAN BE A GAME.

You motivate your preschooler best when you appeal to their desire to play. Whatever the task, turn it into a game; make it fun. When you're having fun, they'll have fun with you. And there is simply nothing more entertaining than the spontaneous laughter of a three-year-old.

THEY HAVE A NEWFOUND CURIOSITY.

Spending time with this phase may seem like a visit to your therapist: "Why?" "Why?" "Why?" But when a four-year-old asks "Why?" they aren't looking for reason or purpose. What they are really asking is "How?" So when they ask you "Why?" the second and third time, remember they aren't doubting you. They're just looking for more of the knowledge they know you must have as an adult person.

IT'S JUST A PHASE SO DON'T MISS IT

OTHER RESOURCES

TO UNDERSTAND MORE ABOUT THE PRESCHOOL PHASE:

BabyCenter.com

Brain Rules for Baby: How to Raise a Smart and Happy Child from Zero to Five by John Medina (Pear Press, 2014)

The Emotional Life of the Toddler by Alicia F. Lieberman (Free Press, 1995)

How to Raise a Child with a High EQ: A Parents' Guide to Emotional Intelligence by Lawrence Shapiro (Harper Perennial, 1998)

Mind in the Making: The Seven Essential Life Skills Every Child Needs by Ellen Galinsky (William Morrow Paperbacks, 2010)

Momtastic.com

Momsoncall.com

Parents.com

Pbs.org/parents

Personality Plus for Parents: Understanding What Makes Your Child Tick by Florence Littauer (Revell, 2000)

Scholastic.com/parents

The Wonder Weeks: How to Stimulate Your Baby's Mental Development and Help Him Turn His 10 Predictable, Great, Fussy Phases into Magical Leaps by Rijt Hetty and Frans X. Plooij (Kiddy World Publishing; Updated edition, 2013)

The Wonder Years by American Academy of Pediatrics (Bantam Books, 2007)

Touchpoints: Birth to Three by T. Berry Brazelton, M.D Joshua D. Sparrow, M.D (Da Capo Press; Second Edition, 2006)

What's Going on in There?: How the Brain and Mind Develop in the First Five Years by Lisa Elliot (Random House Publishing Group, 2000)

WholesomeBabyFood.com

Your Child's Growing Mind: Brain Development and Learning From Birth to Adolescence by Jane Healy (Harmony, 2004)

ZerotoThree.org

POTTY TRAINING RESOURCES:

For potty training suggestions based on your toddler's personality: https://www.pull-ups.com/en-us/potty-training/program/new-way-train-pull-ups-potty-partnership

Oh Crap! Potty Training: Everything Modern Parents Need to Know to Do It Once and Do It Right by Jamie Glowacki (Touchstone, 2015)

Potty Train Your Child in Just One Day: Proven Secrets of the Potty Pro by Teri Crane and Philip Caravella (Touchstone, 2006)

For your potty trainee:

Even Firefighters Go Potty by Naomi Wax & Wendy Wax (Little Simon, 2008)

Everyone Poops by Taro Gomi (Kane/Miller, 2001)

Once Upon a Potty by Alona Frankel (Harper Collins, 1999)

Potty by Leslie Patricelli (Candlewick, 2010)

The Potty Book for Boys / For Girls by Alyssa Satin Capucilli (Barrons, 2000)

Elmo's Potty Time (DVD) (Sesame Street, 2010)

TO HELP YOU LEVERAGE THE PRESCHOOL PHASE BETTER:

Blessings of a Skinned Knee: Using Jewish Teachings to Raise Self-Reliant Children by Wendy Mogel (Scribner, 2008)

Games to Play with Two-Year-Olds by Jackie Silberg (Gryphon House; Revised Edition, May 1, 2002)

Gymboree 365 Activities You and Your Baby Will Love by Roni Leiderman and Wendy Masi

Happier at Home: Kiss More, Jump More, Abandon Self-Control, and My Other Experiments in Everyday Life by Gretchen Rubin (Harmony, 2013)

Legacy Marble App (for Android and iPhone)

MoneyAsYouGrow.org

Mom's On Call Toddler Book by Laura Hunter and Jennifer Walker. Mom's On Call LLC, 2012.

Parenting Is Wonder-full by Sue Miller and Holly Delich (Orange, 2014)

Parent Cue app (for Android and iPhone)

Playful Parenting: A Bold New Way to Nurture Close Connections, Solve Behavior Problems, and Encourage Children's Confidence by Lawrence Cohen (Ballantine, 2001)

Playing for Keeps: Six Things Every Kid Needs by Reggie Joiner and Kristen Ivy (Orange, 2013)

Positive Discipline by Jane Nelsen Ed.D. (Ballantine Books; Updated edition, 2006)

Raising Your Spirited Child: A Guide for Parents Whose Child Is More Intense, Sensitive, Perceptive, Persistent, Energetic by Mary Sheedy Kurcinka (Harper, 2006)

TheParentCue.org

DISCIPLINE RESOURCES:

Love and Logic by Foster Cline and Jim Fay (NavPress, 2016)

No Drama Discipline by Daniel Siegel and Tina Payne Bryson (Bantam 2014)

Personality Plus for Parents: Understanding What Makes Your Child Tick by Florence Littauer (Revel, 2000)

Positive Discipline by Jane Nelson (Ballantine Books, 2006)

FIGHT FOR REST:

Peps.org/ParentResources/by-topic/self-care/self-care-for-parents

Parenting.com/article/take-care-of-yourself-for-a-change-1212610777175

Psychcentral.com/blog/archives/2014/01/05/self-care-strategies-for-busy-moms/

TO HELP YOU CELEBRATE THE PRESCHOOL PHASE:

Celebrations.com

Family Fun Magazine

Parents.com/holiday

The Christmas Story by Autumn Ward (Orange, 2015)

The Easter Story by Autumn Ward (Orange, 2016)

TO HELP YOU NAVIGATE THE PRESCHOOL PHASE:

Joining Children on the Spiritual Journey by Catherine Stonehouse (Bridgepoint Books, 1998)

Simple Truths: A Simple, Natural Approach to Discussing Sex With Your Children by Mary Flo Ridley (Just Say Yes, 2009)

Teaching Your Children Healthy Sexuality by Jim Burns (Pure Foundations, 2008)

AUTHORS

REGGIE JOINER

Reggie Joiner, founder and CEO of the reThink Group, has journeyed through the phases with four kids of his own. He and his wife Debbie raised Reggie Paul (RP), Hannah, Sarah, and Rebekah. Now they have two grandchildren, Abigail and Miles, both in the Zero to One phase at the release of this book.

The reThink Group (also known as Orange) is a non-profit organization whose purpose is to influence those who influence the next generation. Orange provides resources and training for churches and organizations that create environments for parents, kids, and teenagers.

Before founding the reThink Group in 2006, Reggie was one of the founders of North Point Community Church. During his 11 years with Andy Stanley, Reggie was the executive director of family ministry where he developed a new concept for relevant ministry for children, teenagers, and married adults.

Reggie has authored and co-authored ten books including: *Think Orange, Seven Practices of Effective Ministry, Parenting Beyond Your Capacity, Playing for Keeps, Lead Small, Creating a Lead Small Culture*, and his latest *It's Just a Phase So Don't Miss It.*

For more about Reggie, visit ReggieJoiner.com or connect with him on Twitter @ReggieJoiner.

KRISTEN IVY

Kristen Ivy, executive director of messaging at Orange, and her husband, Matt, are in the middle of the preschool phase with a Kindergartener (Sawyer), a preschooler (Hensley), and Raleigh, who is headed into the One and Two Phase at the writing of this book.

Before beginning her career at reThink in 2006, Kristen earned her Bachelors of Education from Baylor University in 2004. She received a Master of Divinity from Mercer University in 2009. She worked in the public school as a high school Biology and English teacher, where she learned firsthand the importance of influencing the next generation.

At Orange, Kristen has played an integral role in the development of the elementary, middle school, and high school curriculums and has shared her experiences at speaking events across the country. Kristen is a co-author of *Playing for Keeps*, *Creating a Lead Small Culture*, and *It's Just a Phase So Don't Miss It*.

You can follow Kristen's work on the Phase project at JustAPhase.com, or connect with her on Twitter @Kristen_Ivy.

FOREWORD
SHERRY SURRATT

Sherry Surratt is the CEO of MOPS International and has also served as Director of Innovation Labs at Leadership Network and as staff pastor at Seacoast Church in Charleston, South Carolina. Sherry is the author of three books: *Brave Mom*, *Beautiful Mess*, and *Just Lead*. She lives in Denver with her pastor husband, Geoff, and has two adult children and two grandchildren. Sherry is a coffee lover, shoe-junkie, and a big fan of moms and women leaders. You can connect with her online at SherrySurratt.com or follow her on Twitter at @SherrySurratt.

HEALTH
DR. JEAN SUMNER

Dr. Jean Sumner is the Assistant Dean for Mercer's School of Medicine. She has practiced internal medicine for the past 30 years in her home state of Georgia with a mission to educate other physicians to meet the primary care and health care needs of rural and medically under-served areas. She has served as hospital chief of staff and nursing home medical director, as well as a board member, chair and president of numerous community and statewide professional organizations. Dr. Sumner lives in Wrightsville, Georgia, with her husband Joseph. She has two grown kids with kids of their own.

SEXUALITY
DR. JIM BURNS

Jim Burns is president of HomeWord and executive director of the HomeWord Center for Youth and Family at Azusa Pacific University. Jim speaks to thousands of people around the world each year. He has over 1.5 million resources in print in over 25 languages. Jim's radio broadcast is heard on over 800 stations a day and heard around the world via podcast at *HomeWord.com*. Some of his books include *Faith Conversations for Families*, *Confident Parenting*, *The Purity Code*, and *Creating an Intimate Marriage*. Jim and his wife, Cathy, and their three daughters live in Southern California.

TECHNOLOGY
JON ACUFF

Jon Acuff is the New York Times Bestselling author of five books including his most recent, *Do Over: Rescue Monday*, *Reinvent Your Work* and *Never Get Stuck*. For 17 years he's helped some of the biggest brands in the world tell their story. He's written for Fast Company, the Harvard Business Review, CNBC and many other national media outlets. In 2010 he used his influence with his tribe to build two kindergartens in Vietnam. Jon lives with his wife, Jenny, and two daughters, L.E. and McRae, in Franklin, Tennessee. You can read more of his work at Acuff.me or on Twitter @JonAcuff.

CONTRIBUTORS

RESEARCH AND DEVELOPMENT TEAM

Sarah Anderson
Sarah Bragg
Elle Campbell
Elizabeth Higgins
Crystal Chiang
Holly Crawshaw
Kathy Hill
Mike Jeffries
Darren Kizer
Brooklyn Lindsey
Cara Martens
Nina Schmidgall
Dan Scott
Deb Springer
Lauren Terrell
Melanie Williams
Karen Wilson

PROFESSIONAL ADVISORS

Sharai Bradshaw MA
Lydia Criss Mays PhD
Jackie Dunagan LMFT
Mallory Even LPMT, MT-BC
Laura Lenz MT-BC
Nicole Manry PhD
Debra McDonald, Ohio Teacher of the Year, 2014
Laura Meyers PhD
Hannah Rinehart MA, LPC, NCC
Deborah Smith MA, LPC
Chinwé Williams PhD, LPC, NCC, CPCS
Jenifer Wilmoth LMFT

CREATIVE CONTRIBUTORS

Anna Aigner-Muhler
Frank Bealer
Jessica Bealer
Abby Carr
Mike Clear
Sam Collier
Ben Crawshaw
Alexa Felice
Amy Fenton
Pam Haight
Elizabeth Hansen
Donny Joiner
Kacey Lanier
Paul Montaperto
Lindsey Needham
Ben Nunes
Brandon O'Dell
Greg Payne
Kevin Ragsdale
Grace Segars
Angie Smith
Melissa Thorson
Colette Taylor
Autumn Ward
Jon Williams

ENDNOTES

1 Tynan, Dan, and Christina Wood. "Your Amazing Baby: 'Wow!'-Worthy Development Facts." *babycenter.com.* 1http://www.babycenter.com/0_your-amazing-baby-wow-worthy-development-facts_10386124.bc.

2 Huelke, Donald F. "An Overview of Anatomical Considerations of Infants and Children in the Adult World of Automobile Safety and Design." Annual *Proceedings/Association for the Advancement of Automotive Medicine* 42:93-113. http://www.ncbi.nlm.nih.gov/pmc/articles/PMC3400202/.

3 Graham, Judith, and Leslie A. Forstadt. "Children and Brain Development: What We Know About How Children Learn." *University of Maine*, 2011. http://umaine.edu/publications/4356e.

4 Nowakowski, Richard S. "Stable Neuron Numbers from Cradle to Grave." *Proceedings of the National Academy of Sciences of the United States of America* 103, no. 33 (August 15, 2006): 12219-20. doi:10.1073.

5 Huttenlocher, Peter R. Neural Plasticity: The Effects of Environment on the Development of the Cerebral Cortex. N.p.: Harvard University Press, 2002.

6 Woolley, J. D. "Verbal–Behavioral Dissociations in Development." *Child Development* 77, no. 6 (2006): 1539-53.

7 Harris, Paul L. "Social Cognition." *Handbook of Child Psychology*, 19th ser., II, no. 4 (June 1, 2007). doi:10.1002/9780470147658.chpsy0219.

8 Piaget, Jean. *The Origins of Intelligence in Children.* New York: International Universities Press, 1952.

9 Gable, Sara, and Melissa Hunting. "Nature, Nurture, and Early Brain Development." *University of Missouri Extension*, 2015. http://extension.missouri.edu/p/GH6115.

10 Healy, Jane. *Your Child's Growing Mind: Brain Development and Learning from Birth to Adolescence.* 3rd ed. New York: Broadway Books, 2004.

11 McKim, Fiona. "10 of the Most Fascinating Toddler Facts." Junior. Last modified March 18, 2014. http://www.juniormagazine.co.uk/baby-and-toddler/10-of-the-most-fascinating-toddler-facts/8795.html.

12 Encheff, Jenna L. "Kinematic Gait Analysis of Children with Neurological Impairments Pre and Post Hippotherapy Intervention." PhD diss., The University of Toledo, 2008.

13 Aetrex Worldwide Inc. "Foot Facts." foot.com. Last modified 2016. http://www.foot.com/site/professional/foot-facts.

14 Hideout, Victoria. "Zero to Eight: Children's Media Use in America." *Common Sense Media*, 2011. https://www.commonsensemedia.org/research/zero-to eight-childrens-media-use-in-america.

15 American Academy of Otolaryngology Head and Neck Surgery. "Ear Tubes." entnet.org. Last modified 2016. http://www.entnet.org/content/ear-tubes.

16 Lathey, Nicholas, Tracey Blake. *Small Talk.* New York, NY: The Experiment, 2013, 157.

17 BabyCenter LLC. "Milestones: 13-24 Months." BabyCenter. Last modified 2016. http://www.babycenter.com/0_milestones-13-to-24-months_1496589.bc.

18 Kadane, Lisa. "Your Toddler's Memory." Today's Parent. Last modified April 17, 2013. http://www.todaysparent.com/toddler/toddlers-memory.

19 "The Laughing Stork's Fun Parenting Facts." The Laughing Stork. Last modified December 12, 2012.http://thelaughingstork.com/blog/2012/12/12/the-laughing-storks-fun-parenting-facts-3/.

20 BabyCenter Medical Advisory Board, ed. "Separation Anxiety." BabyCenter. http://www.babycenter.com/0_separation-anxiety_145.bc.

21 Akron Children's Hospital. "Security Blankets." Akron Children's Hospital. Last modified 2016. https://www.akronchildrens.org/cms/tips/security_blankets/.

22 Fitter, Fawn. "Security Blankets." Psychology Today. Last modified March 1, 2005. https://www.psychologytoday.com/articles/200503/security-blankets.

23 Levine, Madeline. *The Price of Privilege*. New York, NY: Harper Perennial, 2008.

24 Meins, Elizabeth, Charles Fernyhough, Rachel Wainwright, Mani Das Gupta, Emma Fradley, and Michelle Tucker. "Maternal Mind-Mindedness and Attachment Security as Predictors of Theory of Mind Understanding." *Child Development* 73, no. 6 (November/December 2002): 1715-26. http://www.ibl.liu.se/forskarutbildning/forskarkurser-psykologi/utvecklingspsykologi/filarkiv/1.229161/ Meins.pdf

25 Landry, Susan H., Karen E. Smith, Paul R. Swank, and Cathy Guttentag. "A Responsive Parenting Intervention: The Optimal Timing Across Early Childhood for Impacting Maternal Behaviors and Child Outcomes." *Developmental Psychology* 44, no. 5 (September 2008): 1335-53. http://dx.doi.org/10.1037/a0013030.

26 Mendelsohn, Alan L., Carolyn Brockmeyer Cates, Adriana Weisleder, Samantha B. Berkule, and Benard P. Dreyer. "Promotion of Early School Readiness Using Pediatric Primary Care as an Innovative Platform." *Zero to Three*, 1st ser., 34, no.1 (September 2013): 29-40.

27 Thomas, Jennifer. "Potty Training Best Between Ages 2 and 3." ABC News. Last modified January 22, 2016. http://abcnews.go.com/Health/Healthday/ potty-training-best-ages/story?id=9633995.

28 Lewis, Michael, Jeannette M. Havilland-Jones, and Lisa Feldman Barrett, eds. *Handbook of Emotions*. 3rd ed. N.p.: The Guiliford Press, 2010.
29 Bretherton, Inge, Janet Fritz, Carolyn Zahn-Waxler, and Doreen Ridgeway. "Learning to Talk about Emotions: A Functionalist Perspective." *Child Development* 57, no. 3 (June 1986): 529-48. doi:10.2307/1130334.

30 Ibid.

31 Wellman, Henry M., Paul L. Harris, Mita Banerjee, and Anna Sinclair. "Early Understanding of Emotion: Evidence from Natural Language." *Cognition and Emotion* 9, nos. 2-3 (1995): 117-49. doi:10.1080/02699939508409005.

32 Denham, Susanne A., and Elizabeth A. Couchoud. "Young Preschoolers' Understanding of Emotion." *Child Study Journal* 20, no. 3 (1990): 171-92. http://search.ebscohost.com/login. aspx?direct=true&db=psyh&AN=1991-09616-001&site=ehost-live.

33 Dunn, Judy, Inge Bretherton, and Penny Munn. "Conversations about Feeling States Between Mothers and Their Young Children." *Developmental Psychology* 23, no.1 (January 1987): 132-39.

34 Michaelson, Linda, and Michael Lewis. "What Do Children Know about Emotions and When do They Know It?" *The Socialization of Emotions,* 117-39. doi:10.1007/ 978-1-4613-2421-8_6.

35 Brown, Jane R., and Judy Dunn. "'You Can Cry Mum': The Social and Developmental Implications of Talk about Internal States." *British Journal of Developmental Psychology* 9, no. 2 (June 1991): 237-56. doi:10.1111/j.2044-835X.1991.tb00874.x.

36 Wellman, Henry M., and Mita Banerjee. "Mind and Emotion: Childrens' Understanding of the Emotional Consequences of Beliefs and Desires." *British Journal of Developmental Psychology* 9, no. 2 (June 1991): 191-214. DOI:10.1111/j.2044-835X.1991.tb00871.x.

37 Stein, Nancy L., and Linda J. Levine. "The Causal Organisation of Emotional Knowledge: A Developmental Study." *Cognition and Emotion* 3, no. 4 (1989): 343-78. doi:10.1080/02699938908412712.

38 Warren, Heather K., Susanne A. Denham, and Hideko H. Bassett. "The Emotional Foundations of Social Understanding." *Zero to Three* 28, no. 5 (May 2008): 32-39. http://zerotothree.org/site/ PageServer?pagename=ter_journalsingle.

39 Thompson, Ross A. "The Psychologist in the Baby." *Zero to Three* 28, no. 5 (May 2008): 5-12.

40 Charlesworth, Rosalind. *Understanding Child Development*. 9th ed. Belmont, CA: Wadsworth Cengage Learning, 2014.

41 Kraft, Colleen. "Building Brains, Forging Futures: A Call to Action for the Family-Centered Medical Home." *Zero to Three* 34, no.1 (2013): 16-21.

42 Repacholi, Betty M., and Alison Gopnik. "Early Reasoning About Desires: Evidence from 14- and 18-Month-Olds." *Developmental Psychology* 33, no. 1 (1997): 12-21.https://www.bc.edu/content/dam/files/schools/cas_sites/ psych/pdf/critique_desires.pdf.

43 Shapiro, Larwrence E. *How to Raise a Child with a High EQ: A Parent's Guide to Emotional Intelligence*. N.p.: Harper Perennial, 1998.

44 Harris, Paul L. "Social Cognition." *Handbook of Child Psychology*, 19th ser., II, no. 4 (June 1, 2007). doi:10.1002/9780470147658.chpsy0219.

45 Denham, Susanne A. *Emotional Development in Young Children*. New York: Guilford Press, 1998.

46 Raikes, H.A., and R.A. Thompson. "Family Emotional Climate, Attachment Security, and Young Childrens Emotion Understanding in a High-Risk Sample." *British Journal of Developmental Psychology* 24, no. 1 (2006): 89-104.

47 Luby, J.L., C. Mrakotsky, A. Heffelfinger, K. Brown, M. Hessler, and E. Spitznagel. "Modification of DSM-IV Criteria for Depressed Preschool Children." *American Journal of Psychiatry* 160, no. 6 (2003): 1169-72. http://www.ncbi.nlm.nih.gov/pubmed/12777277.

48 Luby, J.L., D.M. Barch, A.C. Belden, M.S. Gaffrey, R. Tillman, C. Babb, and K.N. Botteron. "Maternal Support in Early Childhood Predicts Larger Hippocampal Volumes at School Age." *Proceedings of the National Academy of Sciences* 109, no. 8 (2012): 2854-59. http://www.pnas.org/content/109/8/2854.full.

49 Ibid.,8

50 Hart, Betty, and Todd R. Risley. *Meaningful Differences in the Everyday Experience of Young American Children*. Baltimore: P.H. Brookes, 1995.

51 Oppenheim, D., N. Koren-Karie, and A. Sagi-Schawartz. "Emotion Dialogues Between Mothers and Children at 4.5 and 7.5 Years: Relations with Children's Attachment at 1 Year." *Child Development* 78, no.1 (2007): 38-52. http://www.ncbi.nlm.nih.gov/pubmed/17328692.

52 Laible, D.J., and R.A. Thompson. "Mother-Child Conflict in the Toddler Years: Lessons in Emotion, Morality, and Relationships." *Child Development* 73, no. 4 (2002): 1187-203.

53 High, Pamela C. "Why Should I Read to My Baby: The Importance of Early Literacy." *Zero to Three* 34, no. 1 (September 2013): 41-44.

54 Thompson, Ross A. "The Psychologist in the Baby." *Zero to Three* 28, no. 5 (May 2008): 5-12.

55 The ReThink Group has published three excellent board books by Autumn Ward: *The Creation Story. The Easter Story. The Christmas Story.*

56 Goodman, Miranda, and Michael Tomasello. "Baby Steps on the Road to Society." *Zero to Three* 28, no. 5 (May 2008): 21-25.

57 Shapiro, Larwrence E. *How to Raise a Child with a High EQ: A Parent's Guide to Emotional Intelligence*. N.p.: Harper Perennial, 1998.

58 Hughes, Virginia. "When Do Kids Understand Death?" *National Geographic*. Last modified July 26, 2013. http://phenomena.nationalgeographic.com/2013/07/26/when-do-kids-understand-death/.

59 Academy of Pediatrics. "Sexuality Education for Children and Adolescents." Pediatrics 108, no. 2 (August 1, 2001): 498-502. http://pediatrics.aappublications.org/content/108/2/498.

60 American Academy of Pediatrics. "Media and Children." *American Academy of Pediatrics*. Last modified 2016. https://www.aap.org/en-us/advocacy-andpolicy/aap-health-initiatives/pages/media-and-children.aspx

LOOK FOR NEW PHASE PARENTING RESOURCES AVAILABLE SOON

WWW.JUSTAPHASE.COM